Do It Yourself!

DO IT YOURSELF!

1st edition
© 2012 Bruno Gmünder Verlag GmbH
Kleiststraße 23-26, 10787 Berlin, Germany
info@brunogmuender.com
Original title: Mach's dir!
Stephan Niederwieser © 2006 Bruno Gmünder Verlag GmbH
Translation: David Miller
Layout: Enrico Dreher
Cover art: Dolph Caesar
Cover photo: © Dylan Rosser, www.dylanrosser.com
Printed in South Korea

ISBN 978-3-86787-258-4

More about our books and authors:
www.brunogmuender.com

Stephan Niederwieser

DO IT YOURSELF!

The Complete Guide to Masturbation!

BRUNO GMÜNDER

Stephan Niederwieser *is the author of several novels and numerous short stories, his best selling sex guides have been printed in many editions. He translates from English and Swedish, and has published erotica under the pseudonym Gerke van Leiden. He is also a natural healer and therapist with training in family constellation therapy.*

www.stephan-niederwieser.de

Dear Reader,

This isn't a cook book (surprise!)! Cooking recipes you can follow blindly, because the worst thing that can happen is that you have to chuck it out. Playing with yourself you should never just follow somebody else's suggestion, instead try for yourself, feeling into it, making it your own experience.

In other words: I have tried and tested (to the best of my knowledge and ability) most of the techniques and tools presented here, but every body is different and consequently reacts in different ways. Every cock, every ass, every nipple is an 'individual,' so if a given technique or sex toy is painful or doesn't feel good, abandon it before you injure yourself. To cut to the chase: The author and publisher accept no liability for any harm or damage that might arise as a result of the information provided here. But that was obvious to you anyway, wasn't it? Have fun experimenting!

This book is dedicated to my German and Latin teachers. Oh yes, and my sports teacher too. Mm, mustn't forget my math teacher here, can't forget my biology teacher, and don't want to forget my economics teacher.

Dearest French teacher, thank you for all those lovely classes (although I would have welcomed a little French kissing rather than French irregular verbs). And you too, hairy teacher in the 5th grade, thanks for being my inspiration during all those wonderful hours I spent alone underneath my quilt—what was your name again? And um...I'd also like to thank my physics teacher, with whom I very much enjoyed going swimming—damn, your swimsuit was pretty skimpy! And dear chemistry teacher, you have no idea how happy I was during those minutes spent with you in the shower.

When I look back, maybe school wasn't so bad after all.

"In April," says he, "the whole of nature is in love!
And springtime lends the fields their verdant finery.
Let us love one another! What could be sweeter?
Let us love one another, I beseech you!
Here on earth there is no other happiness in life!"
A tranquil grove emboldens him so,
He seizes a hand, and 'tis in vain I say
"No, enough!"

Jacques Offenbach, *Bluebeard*
(libretto by Meilhac and Halévy)

What's inside

Once upon a time...

Playing with yourself

1 Never be bored again: the basics

2 From lust to a sense of wellbeing

3 Time to get out of bed! Changing places

4 Taking things to a different level: additional stimuli

5 Cumming till they call 911: jacking off for experts

_____Um ... I've just got a few more questions

_____Finding out more

Natural **penis** enlargement program page 170

"Once you understand that, you're no longer embarrassed"

It's no big secret that jerking off is one of the greatest pleasures a man can enjoy, which is why many of us like going to places where we can indulge in this pastime. But emails from many desperate readers tell me that once they've arrived, they often don't have the courage to join the party. I've wondered how this could happen, but since sex parties aren't quite the ideal location for interviewing embarrassed queens I've turned to someone who ought to know: As part of his job porn actor Jack van Dean (▶ www.jackvandean pornstar.com) has to frequently undress in front of strangers.

Even though Jack van Dean loves to take off his clothes...

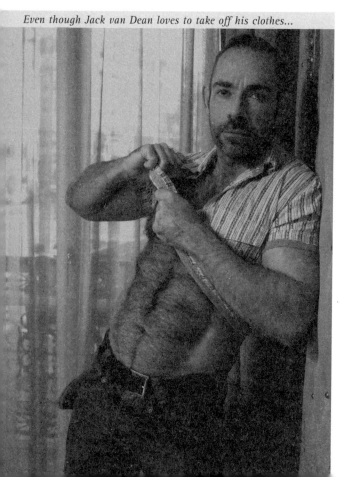

Oh, sure. My God, you can't imagine the drama I went through in school every time I was meant to change for P.E. in front of my fellow students. And even today I'm always the last person to take off his T-shirt when I go dancing.

But you really have nothing to be embarrassed about!

Oh well, I don't always want people to see everything right away. That means there's no surprise later on.

Okay, so that was the excuse you'd give to journalists! What about the real reason?

(Laughs) Okay, I'll tell you the truth, because I know you'll never reveal my secret to anyone: I find it embarrassing to expose myself in front of strangers.

But you do that in your movies, too. And that's only the half of it!

That's different. There's a director, two cameramen, two guys in the lighting crew, and the partners I'm with. People know one another. They're professionals, and all they want is to create a good product. It's a job.

So that means you're simply able to switch off any feelings of embarrassment when you're making a movie?

Um ... *(thinks)*. Well, when Catalina cast me back then they'd only seen my photos. I went along and had to strip to my underwear. That was pretty unpleasant.

But you haven't got an inferiority complex, have you?

Don't even go there! I was doing a movie once, and I'd saved myself for a whole week. The top had a huge cock, uncut, and I was really horny. So I was lying there on my back, and I had to cum first. And wow, my sperm exploded onto my face, my stomach was covered with it, I was really proud of my cumshot. Then the top pulled his cock out of me and ejaculated over my head so it splattered onto the wall.

(Now I'm laughing) So I guess you were pretty frustrated, huh? But I'm sure you've experienced bigger disasters than that.

Yes, of course. I was cast as a top once, yet despite some Viagra and the best will in the world I couldn't get it up—my bottom hadn't washed, and his breath stank. And...my god *(Jack shakes his head)*, when I became a Catalina Exclusive I asked the producer for a guy with a huge cock as a birthday present. He looked really awesome in the movies, and his cock—wowee! I got him. But then this guy turned out to be just a big asshole. We English say: Beware of what you wish for!

Are there many assholes in this profession?

No, it's like anywhere else. I've met some very nice people, too. Most of them only do porn in their spare time. One of them plays the piano for a girls' ballet troupe for his main job, and another is a flight attendant.

How appropriate! But I was actually hoping you'd tell me how to get aroused in spite of strangers looking on, or how to manage once you're aroused. Surely you must have some tricks. Let's have them!

Oh well, in my job as an escort I often have to get myself in the right mood, because of course I'm not exclusively booked by stunningly handsome clients. Fortunately I have very sensitive nipples. That's

...he keeps his pants on at all times

helped me in the past with cumshots in movies. I can usually find something about the other guy that excites me: maybe his ear or his hands. If that doesn't work, I focus completely on myself and play with my nipples. That never fails. At least, almost never.

And if it does?

Then my memories of hot sex help. I couldn't cum when I was filming once, but you don't get paid if there isn't a money shot. So I went into the next room and remembered the hot cock I'd recently had awesome sex with. Then I ran out, lay on the couch and ejaculated.

Aha, so it's the nipples. With Carlo Masi it's his balls. Taoism says you can win a woman's heart with gifts and compliments, but you can win over a man by touching his genitals. Can you confirm that?

(Thinks) Hmm, yes, that's probably true. Sometimes I'm not the slightest bit horny when I'm confronted with a date or a client for the first time—quite the opposite. But as soon as I get physical contact with him, as soon as I can feel him, I get aroused.

So do you prepare yourself for shooting a movie?

I often watch a DVD in the morning. If my cock gets stiff, I just hope it'll work in the afternoon too *(laughs)*.

Let's be serious for a moment. Surely something must help you cope with all these imponderables in your job?

I'm reluctant to say it, because it might destroy the myth of the 'porn star,' but I've never met anyone who's really satisfied with their body. If someone has no complaints about their cock, they think their ass is too fat or they have too little hair on their chest. Everyone has some sort of hang-up. Once you understand that, you're no longer embarrassed to get undressed in front of others or even have sex in their presence.

As a result of his movies (which were also made for Titan, All Worlds and Cazzo), Catalina Exclusive Jack van Dean was placed in the Top 500 by Adams Video Guide. He currently works as an escort in Berlin, London and San Francisco.

Look who's cumming ...

Once upon a time...

When I began to write about sex, I always did it with something nagging at the back of my mind: "Look Honey, everyone's known that for ages. What makes you want to tell gay men about blow jobs?" And people I talked to confirmed my doubts. "Who's gonna buy something like that?" or "So who needs books like that?" were some of the most common objections.

The sales figures have confounded the doubters. A really dumb idea? No way! After ten years, five sex manuals, a pile of articles with sex tips plus countless reader emails, I can give a very precise response to these questions: When it comes to sex, there are at least two types of gay man. Some run around with a megaphone shouting, "I know it all, and anyone who still has any questions is a mere beginner." Others stand to the side and say, "Wow, so all that remains to be discovered!"

Welcome if you're curious, welcome my friend. Welcome, my fellow traveler into the largely uncharted territory of orgasms. Welcome, Reader. I'm glad you're here, because my experiences in strangers' bedrooms demonstrate that the lack of knowledge about male sexuality could hardly be greater. And that applies (albeit not exclusively) to those people who think they know everything. It's lovely to have you here, to greet someone who has the courage to discover new things so they can enjoy broadcasting them to the wider world.

Of course you'd be the perfect audience for a whole load of historical information about one of the nicest ways of getting to know and develop yourself. There are plenty of exciting things to tell you as well, but the problem is there's a limited amount of space in this book. So I want to, indeed have to, restrict myself to the essentials.

If you believe the surveys, 20% of teenage boys are still surprised to wake up in the morning and discover a damp patch on the sheets (a phenomenon quaintly referred to by our Gallic cousins as 'making a map of France'). Even if you listen somewhat more carefully to statements made by quite a few long-serving queers, you'll still be subjected to a number of prejudices—for example, only losers jerk off because they haven't found someone to have sex with. However, before I devote a few words to the all-time favorite myths, let's just take a look at some expressions that are synonymous with this 'sport for the masses.'

▼ Do you still jerk off, or are you wankin' already?

Onanism, masturbation, self-gratification: What am I actually doing?

The simple answer would be: having fun. Or: I'm practicing so I can have better sex in the future. Or: I'm ensuring that my genitals remain in shape and that my mind is awake. But these days it's only facts, facts, facts that matter. So:

The word 'onanism' goes back to the Bible. When Onan's brother Er died, his father Judah told him to impregnate Er's widow in order to continue the family line. However, Onan wanted to be the sole heir of his parents Judah and Shuah, so he politely fucked his sister-in-law but was always careful to withdraw his cock from her pussy before he ejaculated. In Genesis 38:9 it then says that he "spilled it [his seed] on the ground." Onanism therefore describes interrupted sexual intercourse *(coitus interruptus)*. So if someone catches you masturbating in the future and accuses you of onanism (a word that is mostly used by rather bourgeois people), you can puff out your chest in outrage and dismiss this accusation. Who on earth would screw his sister-in-law and then be dumb enough to pull out his cock when he hasn't finished? Really!

Masturbation

Another case where people gladly cite the negative derivation of the word, namely the Latin *manus* (hand) and *stuprare* (defile). However, it's impossible to rule out that the word 'masturbation' is derived as follows: *mézea* (Greek) = 'genitals,' or maybe the prefix *mas-* for 'male' combined with the Latin *turbare* (disturb). After all, "I'm disturbing my penis" sounds much better than "I'm fornicating with my hand," doesn't it? Nevertheless, masturbation might also come from 'turbo': Just change up a gear, and things really start to happen!

Wanking

This is a term which is more popular in Britain than in America, and its derivation is a little uncertain. Of course it might come from the German 'wanken,' meaning to shake, wobble, sway or stagger, but perhaps that's a little fanciful. In any case, we also have 'wanking-pit' (a bed), 'wanker's doom' (the inevitable outcome of excessive self-abuse), 'wank-fest' (communal masturbation, possibly of a com-

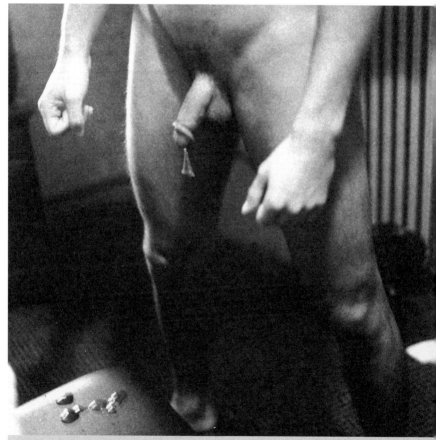

Onanism, jerking off, masturbating: The result is always the same.

petitive nature), and even 'wankalicious,' which means something so awesome it even compares with 'pounding your pud.' There are literally hundreds of other slang expressions, many of them relying on alliteration and/or objects with a phallic appearance, and no doubt a few of them will crop up later on in this seminal work.

Autosexuality

I think the expression 'autosexuality' is pretty cool. Sure, it stands for 'sex with yourself,' although on first hearing it suggests sex in a car. There's also 'autoeroticism' of course, and as Woody Allen famously said: "Don't knock masturbation; it's sex with someone I love."

Self-gratification

To my ears, 'self-gratification' is by far the nicest term since it is totally devoid of negative judgments. After all, there's scarcely anything better than being 'gratified' or 'satisfied.' The term entails just one minor limitation: You're only gratifying yourself, and yet we all know there's nothing more noble than helping another person to achieve satisfaction and gratification.

▼ "Only losers jerk off!"

But they're in good company anyway. The Egyptian sun god Re-Atum felt lonely, so he jerked off into his fist "until it was full of seed" (does that sound familiar to you?). He then drank it and this led to the creation of his son Shu, the god of light and air, as well as his daughter Tefnut, the goddess of moisture.

The famous philosopher Diogenes (399–323 BC) often choked the chicken in broad daylight. When asked why he did it, he replied, "If only I could rub my belly in the same way, so that it was no longer hungry." The ancient Greeks considered it perfectly normal for boys to jerk off under the desk during class.

Synonyms for jerking off

Bashing the bishop	Giving it a tug
Beating your meat	Having one off the wrist
Flogging the log	Playing the skin flute
Spanking the monkey	Polishing Percy in your palm
Buffing the banana	Priming the pump
Varnishing your pole	Playing pocket billiards

And what about the Romans? They hung pendants in the form of stiff peckers around their children's necks in order to protect them from harm. During religious processions, the god Mutunus Tutunus (represented by a large penis decked in flowers) was ceremonially carried through the streets of Rome. Those Romans must have been crazy! Egyptians, Greeks, Romans, architects, philosophers, artists— all complete losers!

One of the most notorious adversaries of masturbation was John Harvey Kellogg, the co-inventor of cornflakes, who wrote the following: "If illicit commerce of the sexes is a heinous sin, self-pollution or masturbation is a crime doubly abominable. As a sin against nature, it has no parallel except in sodomy (see Gen. 19:5, Judges 19:22). It is the most dangerous of all sexual abuses, because the most extensively practiced. The vice consists in any excitement of the genital organs produced otherwise than in the natural way. It is known by the terms self-pollution, self-abuse, masturbation, onanism, manustupration, voluntary pollution, solitary or secret vice, and other names sufficiently explanatory. The vice is the more extensive because there are no bounds to its indulgence. Its frequent repetition fastens it upon the victim with a fascination almost irresistible. It may be begun in earliest infancy, and may continue through life [...] Covering the organs with a cage has been practiced with entire success. A remedy which is almost always successful in small boys is circumcision [...] The operation should be performed by a surgeon without administering an anaesthetic, as the brief pain attending the operation will have a salutary effect upon the mind, especially if it be connected with the idea of punishment, as it may well be in some cases."

"Jerking off gives you bent fingers and makes you go blind!"

Utter nonsense. What sort of logical explanation could there be for this? However, one example of physical atrophy is no myth, but medically proven instead: If you don't jerk off (have regular sex), your weenie will shrivel up.

"Jerking off is only a substitute for proper sex!"

This is something you'll hear again and again, mostly from self-styled 'tough' guys. In the 1960s and 1970s, this even included standard dictionaries which talked about self-gratification as a "transitional phase in puberty." Sexual researchers and urologists are agreed: Masturbation is a discrete form of sex which doesn't replace playing with your partner, and it isn't replaced by the latter either. The masturbation specialist Dr. Harold Litten says: "Self-love is an important basis for mental health!" Sexual researcher Robert Pollack even goes as far as asserting that anyone who doesn't feel the need for a regular rub has a problem. More recent surveys prove that men are even likelier to jerk off if they enjoy a livelier sex life (with their partner). Men who start masturbating early on are subsequently more inclined to pleasure their partners. It's certain that 'going solo' leads to greater familiarity with your own body, which is also a pre-requisite for having fulfilling sex with your partner.

"Sperm must only be expelled in order to create new life!"

I have no intention whatsoever of getting all hot and bothered about antiquated Christian morality. Let's turn instead to another evil in to-day's world: our society's 'performance mindset.' If you were to take the above-mentioned myth seriously, this would be roughly equivalent to saying that you should only eat in order to stay alive. Then what would happen to all those celebrity chefs? 5-course menus aren't really a prerequisite for a healthy diet. And who would then lick a Popsicle or graze on a yummy chocolate bar in between meals?

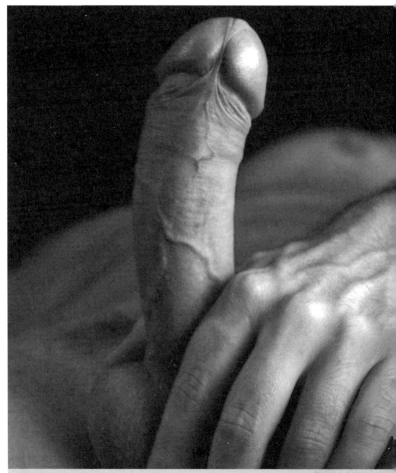

What a shame it would be to reduce such a splendid specimen to merely producing children.

What, I ask you, would become of the enjoyment of eating if you were only allowed to chew apples and muesli?

It's even logical that sexuality ought to go beyond mere procreation. The sociologist Volker Elis Pilgrim explains: "... nature is always primarily interested in the preservation of the individual, then that of living members of the species, and only then the production of offspring."

"Jerking off makes you stupid!"

This is another piece of widespread nonsense. The opposite is true: The hormones that are released when you have sex (adrenaline and cortisol) stimulate the brain and thereby increase creative thinking and the ability to concentrate. Endorphins and serotonin (also known as 'feel-good chemicals') that are released during orgasm strengthen your self-awareness.

"Jerking off is a waste of time!"

Once again, the opposite is true, says Hamburg-based sexual researcher Werner Habermehl: "Sex makes you smart, insofar as you can gather a whole load of life experience that can subsequently be applied in non-sexual areas. The ability to understand sensations and relate to others is increased. That can become an advantage if, for example, you think about business relationships."

▼ Facts that will even persuade your Mom

To summarize, one can say: Jerking off is not only fine, but healthy too. It reduces stress, and the release of hormones strengthens the immune system. You sleep better, your heart and circulation are put through their paces, you lose weight because you burn around 150 calories per ejaculation, your testosterone levels increase (which supports the formation of muscle), and your prostate benefits too: The increased flow of blood prevents inflammation, and pathogens find it harder to establish themselves there because liquids remain in motion.

Jerking off makes you want more; it's considered to be the ideal prerequisite for fulfilled sex with other people, since if you investigate what gives you pleasure you can discover your preferences in a stress-free environment. Last but not least, you don't always have a lover at hand (what an appropriate expression). But even if you do, 'stroking the stallion' is precisely the technique that leads to orgasm in most gay sexual encounters. Therefore: Keep everything in good order! So while we're on the topic...

▼ Cock care

Quite a few people might of course think, "Hey, it's only me playing around down there." Of course I don't want to stick my oar in here, but washing daily ought to be taken for granted. On the other hand, you're overdoing it if you feel the need to wash your weenie after every pee. Too much soap can damage the skin's natural protection shield and, for example, make it more susceptible to fungal infections, i.e. a thin white coating that itches and burns, and not mushrooms (although they'd also get in the way when you are playing around).

Fragrances

Any kind of perfume is a really bad idea in the genital area. Aftershave and eau de toilette contain alcohol which dries the skin and weakens the body's defenses. Moreover, a perfumed cock isn't everyone's cup of tea—and you should always give a little thought to others.

Deodorants are really unhealthy. If your dick still smells bad after you've washed it, you're either not thorough enough or you're suffering from a metabolic disease which you should generally get treated.

While we're on the subject: Faces get peeled and nails are polished, and yet cocks aren't supposed to be beautified? No way! Your trouser snake will truly relish the occasional treat, so apply some (unscented) cream after you've washed it, or even some warm oil.

Burning, itching, straining

I'm afraid I don't have room to list symptoms and illnesses, but you can read about them in my other books (*Bend Over!* and *Blow Me!*). However, that's no substitute for going to the doctor: If you notice any kind of change to your knob (redness, swelling, discoloration, etc.) it's best to go to a doctor who specializes in skin ailments and/ or sexually transmitted infections. Either way you'll sleep better after that. Wouldn't it be a shame if embarrassment or laziness made you miss all those opportunities to make yourself and others happy for the rest of your life?

▼ Inner cock care

So that would be ... massaging the prostate (I don't know why I always have to blurt things out). It's not that I'm pleading for passive anal intercourse here, but seriously, I'm interested in your health ...

A swollen prostate doesn't feel great and it doesn't make you horny either, quite apart from any possible consequences (inflammation, enlargement, cancer). So if you're one of those men who steadfastly refuses to bend over and grit your teeth, it won't do you any harm to occasionally put your finger into your behind and gently massage the little 'nut' in order to mingle the secretions. One minute is enough, and your lower abdomen will feel as good as new.

There are a great many factors which determine how easy it is for you to get an erection and how rigid your cock will be, as well as how long you can last. It's rumored that you won't be able to get it up anymore when you're old, or it will no longer be as hard. This rumor is the most harmful neurotoxin imaginable because it means people think it doesn't matter, and duly indulge in a poor lifestyle. Don't believe it! You should start right away to counteract your 'destiny.'

Poor diet

It's well known that a poor diet leads to deposits in the blood vessels, which can become constricted or blocked. Poor circulation = potential problems in getting an erection: It's as simple as that. Enzymes in food have a preventative effect (pineapple, papaya and mango contain plenty of them), and the same applies to low-fat foods and/ or foods with so-called healthy fats (Omega-3 fatty acids). The latter aren't used to prepare French fries—I just thought I'd mention that. Furthermore, it's no fairy tale that spicy food (Thai, Indian, Arabic ...) enhances your libido, because chili, ginger, etc. stimulate the circulation and clean out the blood vessels.

Poor hydration

The immoderate consumption of alcohol damages the peripheral nervous system, whose main function is to connect the central nervous system to the limbs and organs. This includes the penis! The circulation is slowed down, and problems getting an erection are the consequence (your cock no longer rises as high, it no longer gets as hard, it takes longer to actually excite its tired old head). By contrast, a high fluid intake is important. However, that doesn't mean coffee or black tea (they're both diuretic), but water, green/red teas and fruit juices instead (because then your own sperm will taste better too).

Poor breathing

Nicotine is a neurotoxin. When you smoke a cigarette, your body temperature falls by up to one degree centigrade, which won't exactly have a positive influence on your ability to get an erection.

Poor movement

The process of human civilization has had some pretty dire consequences, and it can be very hard to fight against them. But please don't think I'd like us all to go back to the jungle; there wouldn't be enough room in any case. Daily mouse-clicking or raising the odd potato chip to your mouth isn't enough to keep you fit. Swimming and jogging improve your condition, thereby ensuring more profound orgasms and shorter breaks until the next one; they promote the circulation and thus increase potency. Deliberately building up

I told you to get moving – and I didn't just mean your thumb, you lazybones!

your butt and your leg muscles helps to prevent rapid exhaustion (when you're fucking). It has other benefits too, particularly if you're planning to expose your naked ass to the world in a pair of chaps.

When it comes to everything that's written here, remember that prevention is always preferable to treatment—and not only once erectile dysfunction has already materialized.

You think all this isn't necessary because we have Viagra, etc. now? Um ... perhaps I should point out that there haven't been any longitudinal studies yet. For a 60-year-old who starts using Viagra today, it's of little relevance whether the erectile tissue in his penis will be battered and torn in 10 years' time. It's a different matter if we're talking about a 25-year-old, although very few people seem to give that any thought.

▼ Psychological cock care

People are keen to ignore the fact that it isn't only the cock that requires careful treatment, but the mind too. Good sex relies upon a healthy attitude, so anyone who's ashamed of his needs and desires will find it hard to translate them into action. Indeed, such people may require drugs or dark locations to actually make them a reality, which isn't the ideal launchpad for a healthy, fulfilled, enriching sex life.

That doesn't mean you constantly have to reveal your genitals to the public gaze or interrupt every discussion with "Tell me, have you ever tried sitting on a tennis ball while you're jerking off?" Anyone who behaves in an inappropriately 'uninhibited' manner is just as trapped as any closet queen.

I don't want to create a list of 12000 rules of behavior here, but merely encourage you to take better notice of your reactions. Just pay attention. Do you blush if someone in your group talks about sex? Do you feel ill at ease? Do you start to giggle? Do you deny jerking off if a friend mentions it to you? Pay attention to your reactions, and at all times ask yourself what feels 'awkward' and 'limiting,' and what might help you feel more liberated or even free.

Don't forget: You have a right to self-gratification! You have a right to sex, no matter which religion you belong to. It doesn't matter what your parents, friends, or teachers say about it. And jerking off doesn't harm your health or lead you away from the path of righteousness, let alone to hell!

Once you feel at ease with yourself, the next stage would be to actually discuss it with some good buddies, simply because they might have some techniques you don't know about. After all, it'd be a shame if you missed out on that. At the same time it's a splendid opportunity to dazzle them with everything you've learnt from my books.

Last but not least: The more you value yourself (strong self-confidence, healthy self-esteem, friendly self-love), the likelier it is that you'll aim for a healthy lifestyle. This naturally works the other way round: The more you aim for a healthy lifestyle, the more self-confident you'll become. Your self-esteem gets bigger and thus (you've already guessed what I'm going to write, haven't you?) so does your cock.

Playing with yourself

Taking time, relaxing, getting wet – and everyday life becomes bearable.

I'm sure you found out long ago how to beat your meat. Most people these days learn that really early on; surveys have supposedly discovered that, on average, boys start masturbating when they're 12¾ years old. They generally discover for themselves that their pee-pee is suitable for other things too, i.e. not merely holding it over the toilet and letting it run. However, jerking off is generally not something that people are taught; indeed, it's not even discussed in a major way (even among gay men, who always claim to be very progressive when it comes to sex). This means that masturbation often remains something that happens in secret at night under the sheets—where it must be accomplished as quietly as possible and without getting caught. The consequences of this are:

1. People stick with the first technique that was halfway successful.
2. They do it quickly.
3. They try to avoid making any noise.

And then everyone wonders why there's such a demand for porn movies! Now, if you're not self-sufficient in this respect, you might need some outside stimuli. But we'll do our best to change that right now.

___Never be bored again: the basics

This section deals with what most men do anyway—although due to the above-mentioned circumstances, unfortunately it's often unimaginative or insufficiently varied, which is why boredom sets in. The purpose of this section is therefore to present you with lots of different holds and techniques so that you can expand your repertoire. Maybe one or another of them will be more effective, or help you to experience masturbation more intensely in unusual situations.

I've summarized the names of the techniques and holds in boxes so that you can easily remember them later on. After all, it's hard to leaf hurriedly through a book if you have lube in one hand and a dildo in the other. By the way, you'll be relieved to know that the pages of this book have been treated with a state-of-the-art coating (based on nanotechnology) to prevent them from sticking together.

Your first time

I guess it's rather unlikely that you're doing it for the first time, because lots of people tend to discover their body rather than learn to read, but I don't want to leave anyone out in the rain. So: Welcome to the club! The initiation ritual is as follows:

Make sure you won't be disturbed, so climb up to the attic, go down to the coal cellar, or snuggle up to the hens in the coop, and ensure that no beeping cell phone or curious eyes will disturb this sacred moment. Don't tell anyone about it; you'll only encourage curiosity and provoke trouble-makers. Moreover, other people's prejudices might confuse and influence you as you embark on this amazing journey. This moment belongs to you and you alone; you have the right to awaken the desire within your body, to coax sensual delights from within, and bring yourself to orgasm. No law and no person (not grandma, nor the priest, nor the biology teacher) can prevent you from doing so. If someone nevertheless tries to spoil your fun, seek help. At the end of this book you'll find a list of places that can give you advice and support.

And now for the most important thing: Have a cloth handy! If you're old enough to squander some sperm (kind of 12, 13, 14 onward), you should have something to wipe it off with afterwards.

Are you sitting comfortably? Is it warm enough, so you won't freeze? Is it quiet enough, so you won't be distracted? Good. Now you're ready for action. Allow yourself to be guided by your body. The quickest way to get aroused is by playing around with your principal private parts, namely your cock and balls, but don't restrict yourself to that. As soon as it starts to tingle somewhere, stroke other parts of your body too in order to arouse them. Your nipples are crying out for attention – why else would Nature have made them so prominent? Armpits aren't quite as conspicuous, but they're still very sensitive when touched. Likewise your thighs, the backs of your knees, the entire area underneath (or behind) your balls, and right into your ass. Let's move on to the ...

▼ Positions

Circumstances occasionally dictate the position in which you can play around with yourself. You won't exactly be able to practice your acrobatics if you're camping overnight and are surrounded by a crowd of snoring Boy Scouts, although ... perhaps I need to give that a bit more thought.

On your back

You lie on your back and rub one out. By the way, that's how more than two thirds of all men prefer to do it; roughly 10% respectively do it standing or on their knees, while the rest lie on their stomach. But enough of this tedium! You could also try ...

Rock-a-bye baby

Raise your legs as if you were wanting to shove something into your backside, and then pass your hand behind and between your legs and grab your prick. Or draw your feet closer to your butt so that your knees are raised; keep your feet together, but let both knees fall to either side. When you cum you can then bring your knees together, and even use them as a natural pump in order to direct blood (and energy) from your lower abdomen into your entire body.

Sitting

For example, on a chair. However, one disadvantage here is that your cock is shorter in this position because its base is pulled into your groin. It's not ideal either that your pants start to pinch unless you pull them all the way down beforehand. Moreover, when the sperm duly splashes onto them it'll leave nasty stains which will attract disapproving glances from Mom (or your secretary or partner). Nevertheless: Precisely because this position is rather tricky, the ensuing sense of triumph is all the greater if you can get in the swing of things and actually pull it off.

A propos swinging: Of course sitting is a fabulous position if you occasionally like to hang a couple of weights from your nuts. What, that's new to you? Well then, you can look forward to some really enjoyable games ... but more about that later on.

Let's go back to the sitting position: It's definitely worth trying it out, because what are you supposed to do if you're in the car and you've just received a hot text message? (If nobody ever sends you them, it's high time you recruited a couple of obliging fuck buddies). If you're sitting on a chair you can also spread your legs and feel what that's like!

Sitting on the floor during your coffee break isn't quite so simple, unless you're an author and you have the whole office to yourself. Sitting on the floor has the crucial disadvantage that you're bound to get your necktie dirty. Or is your sperm under such high pressure that you can ejaculate directly into your mouth? If you try it cross-legged that'll definitely help to delay ejaculation. More about that in the section on 'delay techniques.'

Squatting

If you get into the mood while hiking through the forest, you can always say, "Hey Pop, why don't you go ahead, I've just found an awesome mushroom!" Unfortunately you have to undress to do this because your pants will otherwise make it difficult to move your legs. So squat down, spread your legs as wide as possible, and off you go. Alternatively you can grab your cock by passing your hand(s) under and between your legs, and that way you'll simultaneously be spanking your balls as you jerk off. Sexy!

Try it initially without moving your legs at all, i.e. no gyrating your butt or bobbing up and down, or whatever suggests itself. Concentrate fully on your cock. It's a marvelous way of strengthening your calf and buttock muscles without paying for a personal gym instructor. Pretty strenuous, eh? Likewise cumming, but that's precisely the kick you get out of this position. And the "Oooaaaaah-hhh!" when you nevertheless manage it will be all the more heartfelt.

Lying down: comfortable, but maybe not always the most exciting position.

If you think this is a really dumb position, just suggest a better one where you can ride a dildo at the same time. Don't try telling me, "I can shove it in while I'm standing up and brace the dildo against the sink." What if there isn't one nearby? You see!

One subtle side effect: You'll be strengthening your PC muscle, which is extremely important if you're going to have good sex. PC muscle? Okay, okay, just wait until later. Wow, how impatient are you?

On your side

You should practice jerking on your side because it's useful if you've forgotten the paper towels before you go to bed but are too lazy or horny to get up again (don't worry, the bedside rug will be dry again by the morning. Oh, you didn't know why some people have these things lying beside their bed? Good grief!). It's even more exciting if you can't use your normal jerking hand because you (or your partner) are lying on it. And not least of all, you should see the bigger picture and consider that on another occasion you might want to be fucked in this position (it relaxes you and makes penetration easier). If you haven't got an anal orgasm handy right now, you might want to have one off the wrist ...

On all fours

Jerking on all fours is also part of the standard repertoire—if you're doing the 69 position with another guy and blowing him off, or you're getting fucked. Yeah, yeah, I know you're not passive. None of us are *(rolls eyes)*. But you might suddenly crave a good seeing-to doggy-style, so then jerking on all fours should be a cinch. The main problem with all this is how strong you are: Can you jerk for half an hour, supported on just one hand? Great, you won't need to go to the gym then, will you?

On your stomach

You might not believe me, but it works pretty well if you're lying on your stomach. Lie on top of your stiff cock and rub back and forth on it until it gets moist. At the same time, that's the crucial drawback of this position: Your freshly laundered sheets will be as hard as planks after just a few days. Laying plastic bags underneath doesn't work that well because they crackle in a fairly unerotic way and are constantly sliding around. But you can easily include this variation shortly before the annual changing of the bed linen.

Alternative: a rubber sheet (cheaper: pond liner from the DIY store), nice warm lube underneath, and wowee! By using lube you can also avoid getting your nice bushy tummy fur tangled up in your foreskin (if you've got one). You can also put your hands between the bed and your cock; that's preferable for anyone with a long foreskin. Nevertheless, that doesn't necessarily prevent the subsequent mess with the cum.

Kneeling

Different positions mean that different muscle groups are tensed, and that in turn alters the flow of energy during orgasm. That's why you should occasionally try it on your knees for the sake of variety. If not before, this is a technique you'll need if you're wanting to give someone a blow job in a changing cubicle. You can try different positions here too, from kneeling 'upright' to sitting back on your ankles. Ultimately you have to adapt to the height of the person you're with.

In this position you can also put one hand between your legs and beat your meat while the other one can easily reach your scrotum and asshole. If that's too tiring and you want to take the strain off your upper body, you can rest your head on the floor, the bed, or a chair. With a little practice you'll easily be able to spurt into your face.

Sitting on the side of your knee (side saddle or like the Little Mermaid statue in Copenhagen) is not only chic but an interesting alternative. If kneeling is painful for you, use one arm to support yourself on a chair—a slave's back is just as effective in case of emergency.

Backward somersault

The more flexible among us might also attempt a backward somersault: Lie down, fold your legs over your head and place them next to your ears. That's pretty exhausting for an old guy like me, but in my younger days ... If you can't manage that, support yourself by placing your feet against the wall and you're sure to have sperm flying into your face. Or your mouth (gulp).

"I love jerking off!" says Lars, and promptly ejaculates onto the camera.

Standing up

Before things get too complicated, you shouldn't forget that it ought to work standing up too. If not before, this is called for when you first have sex in a tea room (i.e. a public restroom), in the park, or when you're standing in line at the job center. So practice, practice, practice.

Do you still need a reason why the repertoire contains so many positions? Heavens, you never know where you'll end up, and if you're not an expert you'll miss lots of opportunities. In a sauna you might have to manage it with one foot on the bench to protect your stiff dick from prying eyes. You think it's impossible to jerk off in other people's company without them noticing? That's something else you'll learn, so keep on reading ('The Dead Man').

Positions

On your back	Squatting
Rock-a-bye baby	On your side
Sitting	On all fours
Sitting on a chair	On your stomach
Sitting on the floor	Kneeling
With your legs spread	Backward somersault
Side saddle	Standing up

▼ Holds

You can use a variety of holds in each of the positions listed above. Here's a small selection, although it by no means claims to be exhaustive. It's only meant to inspire you to find some more (maybe even under a stranger's duvet?).

One-finger method

Hold your cock firmly in one hand, and use just one finger of the other hand to massage the delicate area of skin that links the glans to the shaft until you ejaculate. Precum, spit or lube make it a more agreeable experience.

Two-finger method

With the two-finger method you grasp your cock between your fingers like a spring roll, croissant or flute. Because this hold only covers a small area of your dick it allows you considerable scope for rubbing, and what's more you can be much more selective about how much pressure to put on your weenie than, for example, if you were using your fist. This can be extended to three or five fingers, depending on the length of your cock.

Ring method

The ring method requires you to form a circle ('OK sign') with your thumb and index finger, thereby enclosing your doodle. This is even suitable for very small willies—but that doesn't mean you should ignore it if you've got a donkey dick. This method imitates (albeit somewhat inadequately) the feeling of pushing through a tight sphincter (ass).

The hook

Form a hook with your index finger and place it around your cock. The backs of the other fingers massage the top of the shaft.

The thumb

Instead of wrapping your fist around your stiff cock, fold your thumb inward so that the upper side of the first joint is lying on the upper side of your cock.

Chopsticks

Place your index finger on the underneath of your cock and your middle finger on the upper side, and jerk it like that.

The 'prick' hold

Instead of always rubbing dutifully up and down, you can also position your hand on your cock so that your fingers are pointing toward your body. If you now move your hand down your cock, you'll be 'pricking' into the tissue around the base of your cock. For small wieners in particular, this is a good way to feel that you've got a longer cock.

Is it a good idea to jerk over the glans? Only you can decide.

The fist

Grasp your cock as if you were gripping a baseball bat. Push the closed hand (which is more or less a fist) back and forth along your shaft. This hold offers maximum contact when rubbing, which for most people means maximum pleasure. However, it only works well if your dick is much longer than the width of your hand.

The double fist ...

... presupposes small hands and/or a long hosepipe. Form a fist with both hands, place one on top of the other, and insert your prick.

Backhand

Then there's the backhand. That may be slightly perverse if it reminds you of tennis (goddammit, you're supposed to be reading a sex manual), but it's really not that odd at all. Grasp your cock as if it were a tennis racquet, and make sure the glans is sticking out from the back of your hand. This way you can comfortably jerk out of the side of your bed, a technique that should be mastered by anyone who spends their nights in dorms. But don't forget to mop up before your fellow student slips on it during the night and breaks his neck.

The belly rubber

If you lie on your back you can place your stiff cock on your stomach and rub up and down on it as if you were rubbing away a stomach ache. It's a good technique if you want to conceal your jerking from someone who's sleeping with you. Hairy stomachs might appreciate some lube. You can get more pressure by using two hands at once, or one on top of the other; alternatively you can use the area of soft skin on the inside of your elbow. These were the first holds I discovered in kindergarten at the tender age of five, thereby enabling me to jerk off without anyone realizing.

The jerk-off prayer

One admirable option is to arrange your hands as if you were praying and push your cock between them. You can produce a variety of stimuli, depending on whether you place your thumbs on the side or wrap them around your cock; how firmly you squeeze can also make a difference.

Holds

1 finger	The 'prick' hold
2 fingers	The fist
3-5 fingers	The double fist
The ring	Backhand
The hook	The belly rubber
The thumb	The jerk-off prayer
Chopsticks	

▼ Techniques

Each of these holds can be adapted in a variety of ways. Firstly, you can use different amounts of pressure (if you've ever been jerked off you'll know that everyone does it differently). Secondly, the speed with which you rub is very important. I've been a (very slow) jerker from an early age. The first man I ever jerked off became impatient pretty quickly and removed my hand from his cock and rubbed it so energetically that it made me dizzy. Henceforth I knew you could also do it at supersonic speed. And it wasn't long before I placed myself in the hands of an Iranian guy who not only blew with great dedication, but also mastered a kind of vibrator technique. He jerked at the speed of light, and it was really hot.

Slowness and speed, both have their advantages. Going slowly promotes awareness; you notice sensations more precisely. I also find you perceive more of the rest of your body. The quick-rub method requires more strength and therefore has something very masculine, hot, animal and powerful about it. It's not a dumb idea to use a mixture of the two either: Rub vigorously until just before the explosion, then change down a gear to super-slow. The minute the arousal subsides, it's full steam ahead once more—by the way, it's a good way of learning how to control your ejaculation (more about that later on).

The rodeo jerk

Sounds mega-butch, and combines the best of both worlds. Rub quickly a couple of times and then go real slow for a few strokes before once again shifting up a gear. It's especially hot if you're jerking off over someone and he's looking up at you from below. It makes you super-masculine, and it also allows you to control your arousal curve magnificently.

Wu Hsien

The legendary Tantra master Wu Hsien passed the following technique on to his disciples, the idea being to achieve control over one's arousal curve. On average, gay men cum after the 54th back & forth stroke, so this exercise is a real challenge:

"Jerk shallow" (i.e. quickly) three times, then once slowly, then repeat that 81 times. Then jerk five times quickly and once slowly, and repeat that 81 times too. And finally, jerk nine times quickly and once slowly—81 times again.

To recover from that, just unscrew your cock and place it in a soothing oil bath.

The wave

Let's use your imagination: Think about the sea rippling away nicely and slowly getting higher and higher until some big waves crash onto the shore. Then they recede and ebb away once more. That's what you should do with your penis too. Rub it gently and softly, just like the sea licking placidly against the shore. But then a storm approaches. Just as the waves get bigger and bigger, you should increase your jerking, take it to higher and higher levels: jerk harder, quicker, and more firmly. Then once you've reached the climax (without cumming!), slowly reduce it again. Play like this with differing storm strengths and wind speeds. If you now set yourself against the storm, i.e. you jerk slowly and gently whenever you're very aroused (and vice versa), the tidal wave will eventually overwhelm you totally.

Happiness can come in tight packages:
You don't always have to be naked to jerk off ...

The glans jerk-off

However, it's not only the speed that can be varied. While some people absolutely need to be jerked firmly over the glans (i.e. the full length of their cock), others can't bear it (modesty forbids that I should talk about myself, but I'm an example of that). This means you should try out different 'stroke lengths,' because they allow you to easily shift down a gear (and moderate your arousal) in spite of going at top speed. Above all, you ought to master this when we subsequently move on to discuss delay techniques, or you want to cum at the same time as someone who isn't as ready to spurt as you are.

Milking

Instead of jerking toward the body, you jerk away from it. It's not very exciting to begin with, but it's worth practicing because it has two immediate advantages: Firstly, it takes longer this way before you cum. Secondly, if you combine this technique with the back-handed ring method (see above) it'll help your cock to get bigger.

The Florentine method

Pull your (fore)skin back firmly to the base of your penis so that your cock rears up a bit more without hurting. This not only makes it slightly harder; if you're sufficiently aroused, it can make you cum on its own—without rubbing at all. I used this technique in school before I was able to produce any sperm, and it worked pretty damn quick for me. Nevertheless, it requires patience and concentration—ideal if you're keen on the math teacher. One tip for the sociology class: The Florentine method is much favored by prostitutes when they want customers to cum faster. This hold also helps when you're fucking and you want to make your cock harder, which can be very useful (especially when confronted with a very tight asshole).

The glans rubber

You pull back the skin 'Florentine-style' and then rub the palm of your other hand over the incredibly engorged and bright red/purple glans (wherever possible using fabric or the soft side of Velcro). Your "Oooh" will quickly change into an "Oooo-aaaah-grrr"!

Massage technique

For the massage hold, grip the base of your cock with one hand and place the other around your pride and joy like a sleeve (fist hold). Then move up the shaft and over the glans, open your hand, and stroke it with the palm of your hand. Then grasp your cock 'back-handed' and slide down the other side of the shaft again. Do the same in reverse. If you're not a precummer, smear some lube onto your cock.

Through your pants

When my ex got circumcised he wasn't supposed to play with himself until everything had healed properly (it takes weeks). But we couldn't wait for that, so he stimulated his glans through his underwear, especially the particularly sensitive part between the urethra and foreskin, keeping the rest of his dick perfectly still (he had no choice). Sure enough, he almost shot a hole through the fabric. Of course no need to get circumcised for this. Stimulate your knob until it's erect, then fondle the head with your fingers until it spurts. This is a good technique for boring meetings at work because it's inconspicuous—apart from the primal screams and your body's epileptic twitches.

Variation: Just stroke the edge of the glans and completely avoid the head. Besides all that, you can also do all of this as an accompaniment to wanking off with the aid of a different technique.

The brush technique

Or: Have you ever brushed your glans? Okay, I realize it's not covered in thick curly hair (or is it?), but this can trigger a really great sensation. Some soft Velcro is ideal, while real tough guys also use a toothbrush for this purpose—electric if possible.

The earthquake

Encircle your cock with the ring hold, but don't rub up and down the shaft. Just move your wrist instead so that your cock swings back and forth, and find the speed that produces the greatest friction. A certain length of cock is required for this.

...and tight jeans can be exciting too

The deep hole

Place the 'fist' on the glans and push it back slowly along the shaft until you reach the base. Meanwhile, lay the other hand (formed into a fist) on the glans and now push it back along the shaft, then repeat this with the first hand, and so on. Lube makes this technique more bearable, so let's just see how long you can keep it up.

The Vulcan salute

Smear plenty of lube onto your cock and balls, also ensuring that your jerking hand is slippery, especially the skin between your middle and ring fingers. Now form your hand to imitate the Vulcan salute made famous by Mr. Spock (Star Trek), place your stiff cock between your middle and ring fingers, and off you go. If you now fondle your balls with the other hand you'll discover worlds where no man has gone before.

Let it ride

For this you will need the edge of a bathtub (unfortunately not accessible to everyone). Mount it as if you were riding a bicycle, then lay your dick along the edge. This is more suitable for soft, flaccid penises. Thick, rock-hard truncheons will hurt; believe me, I've tried it. If you've got a furry belly, your hair will tend to get caught under your foreskin (if you have one), but applying lube to your stomach prevents too many tangles.

Handstand

This is nice too: Do a handstand on something soft and support yourself against the wall. You might get pretty dizzy or even black out when you reach orgasm, so nothing, least of all a glass coffee table, should be in the way to injure you when you finally slump down.

The fuck jerk

An orgasm definitely feels totally different if it's not only your hands that are slaving away, but if you make use of your entire body (hip muscles) instead. Liberally apply lube to one hand, lay a towel underneath you on the bed, place your stiff cock into the slippery hand, then lie on top of it and hold onto the bedframe with the other hand. You can then fuck your own hand.

The elbow

Place your stiffy inside your elbow, bend your arm so that your cock is nice and tight, and off you go. If you do it standing up you can spare your arm muscles and use your whole body instead. Try it with lube too.

The windshield wiper

Smear lube onto your stomach, place your hard prick on top of it and rub it back and forth like a windshield wiper.

Scandinavian

Kneel down, and then sit on a cushion with your bent legs to the right or left of you. Smear some lube onto your thighs and bend your upper body forward; you'll be able to fuck your thighs with your stiff cock. Connoisseurs squeeze their balls between their thighs and calves so that they're simultaneously stretched with every up and down movement of the upper body.

The homemade blow job

You can of course insert your cock into a well-lubed hand and then pull it out. Depending on whether you relax or squeeze your fingers, it feels like a mouth or ass you're fucking. Similar at least. Okay, nothing like it really. But it's still hot.

Thrusting

Place the palm of your hand on your glans and wrap your fingers around your cock (pointing down toward the base); the thumb lies on top, the middle and ring fingers underneath, and there's one finger respectively to the right and left of the shaft. If you now fuck your hand you'll constantly be pushing against the palm of your hand. The glans is stimulated and you'll definitely end up with jizz on your fingers.

The Dead Man #1

All you have to do now is learn how to jack off without anyone nearby noticing. What's the point of that? Well, you might want to do it in company, and you've realized it's not much fun ending up in jail as a result. Stand in front of a mirror. If it reflects the whole of your body, simply lose the lower section so you can only see your arm down to your elbow. Then try the above-mentioned techniques, one after the other, and discover the one that achieves your objective fastest and/or most reliably. Keeping your arm fully in view, you'll be able to adapt the technique so nobody will register the movement of your hand / lower arm. Done! Now you need to learn how to cum without howling like a wolf, rolling your eyes, or fidgeting uncontrollably as if you were plugged into an electrical socket.

Techniques

The rodeo jerk	The deep hole
Wu Hsien	The Vulcan salute
The wave	Let's play gee-gees
The glans jerk-off	Handstand
Milking	The fuck jerk
The Florentine method	The elbow
The glans rubber	The windshield wiper
Massage technique	Scandinavian
Through your pants	The homemade blow job
The brush technique	Thrusting
The earthquake	The Dead Man #1

Using plenty of lube is particularly advisable if you're cut.

▼ Lubricants

I've often been laughed at when I pulled out the lube for jerking, so I'd like to tell you a little tale: Andreas (former monk!) wanted to have hot wax dripped onto his balls. However, he was very anxious about this, so I applied some oil to protect the skin. As I did so, some weird noises suddenly began to emerge from his throat; his small, crooked cock reared up wildly, and Andreas' gaze suddenly seemed lost in a far-off reverie. To cut a long story short: Never before had another person managed to jack Andreas off—until this well-greased moment. He at least has never laughed at me since.

Some techniques I've already written about feel better with lube. However, it goes without saying that it doesn't hurt to learn the difference between dry and wet jerking with other techniques and holds. Nevertheless, don't be satisfied with the first bottle of olive oil that comes to hand, the one your aunt Daisy brought back from her vacation in Italy. You can experiment with fatty/greasy substances such as butter and margarine, or Nivea and professional lubes based on water, oil, or silicone. Fatty/greasy substances feel warmer than water-based lubes, and this is something you can meaningfully exploit to suit the weather, your location or your sexual practice. Silicone-based lubes leave a silky effect on the skin and don't dry out for ages, which may be great when you're fucking but a major disadvantage later on—especially if it's a long way home. They also ruin the bed linen or can only be removed from the floor by using scouring creams. So it's a good idea to be aware of the properties of different lubes so you can reach for the right one during close combat (when fucking is imminent).

▼ Materials

Once you've attempted a variety of techniques, just try them with rubber, leather or woolen gloves; it'll seem like you're doing it for the first time. Alternatively you can pull a sock over your dong, or maybe a freezer bag, or—really classy—bubble wrap (the stuff they pack fragile objects in). And that in turn feels different every time if you previously apply lube to these materials.

▼ Better orgasms

The orgasm is defined as the climax of sexual arousal. The word supposedly comes from the Greek *orgasmos* meaning 'swelling,' 'become ripe' or 'be lustful.' There's a persistent rumor in the Western world that (for a man) it's accompanied by ejaculation, although it doesn't have to be that way. This link is only made by the many people whose first experiences are based on an orgasm where they produced sperm, and who hitherto haven't had the opportunity to experience anything else.

On average, the orgasm lasts for only 3 to 8 seconds, and is often accompanied by complex physical and mental reactions: involuntary muscle contractions, an accumulation of blood in the genital area, increased heart rate and breathing, a sense of euphoria, exhaustion, cries for help, and even proposals of marriage. How the orgasm is experienced depends on many factors: the underlying mood, the gap between it and the most recent orgasm, your personal attitude toward sexuality, the technique you use, the duration of the arousal phase, any aids you might have used to achieve arousal (another person, porn movies, a vibrator), and the type and quantity of any previously consumed drugs. Some people experience ecstasy or go into some kind of trance, while others remain still and silent. The sexual arousal curve subsequently falls off steeply if you ejaculate. On the other hand, if you can experience an orgasm without ejaculation you'll gain energy and strengthen the organism.

Oh, there's just one more thing (to quote the late Peter Falk), and I suppose it's a rather unwelcome piece of news: Men who are fit achieve orgasm with a lower pulse rate and experience it more intensely. By contrast, couch potatoes have to struggle to even reach it, and they're totally exhausted afterwards (so let's take a break while I go jogging round the block).

Anyone who wants to know more about orgasms would do well to look at the corresponding article on Wikipedia, which points out that 'it is possible for men to achieve an orgasm through prostate stimulation alone.'

▼ What should I do with the sperm?

This is a vital question which is often asked far too late because it may seem peripheral during the thrill of arousal—that is until you find the stuff splattered all over your nice clean suit. It's advisable to always have a couple of hankies nearby so you don't end up in trouble when you're standing at the McDonald's parking-lot. However, thin tissues can disintegrate and stick to your dick, which is a rather unpleasant sight.

Having some nice absorbent paper towels next to your bed may be very practical from a housewife's perspective, but maybe it lacks a bit of style. And the smooth transition from lounge to bedroom might be unnecessarily traumatic for your typical one-night stand if he has to negotiate his way past a pile of fly-infested Kleenex waiting to be thrown in the trash can.

I recommend hiding a small, unobtrusive cum towel under the pillow, or even under the quilt; it can then magically appear when required. The general consensus appears to be that towels should be laundered surreptitiously after a decent interval, or thrown away once they become 'grungy', 'gross' or 'crusty'. You should also bear in mind that sperm is one of the most nutritious protein cocktails in the highly competitive market of muscle-building compounds, but as my mother warned me when I was a little boy: "Never accept gifts from strangers!"

By contrast, consuming your own juices isn't harmful at all. Quite the opposite. Once you understand the kind of energy that's required for every ejaculation, you'll follow the advice offered by the mahatmas (Hindu sects) and gladly re-ingest what has been so laboriously expelled from your yogurt slinger—so long as you don't have to lick it off the floor of a public restroom.

What you always wanted to know about sperm

▶ Approx. 5% of the total ejaculate originates from the testicles and epididymis; 45-80% comes from the seminal vesicles; 10-30% from the prostate; and 2-5% from the Cowper's glands (which produce the delectable precum).

▶ On average, men produce 2-6 milliliters every time they shoot their load; each milliliter of ejaculate contains at least 20 million seminal filaments which swim around at a speed of 1-4 mm/min—after they've been catapulted out in 3−10 batches, at approx. 40 km/h (25 mph).

▶ The main ingredient is fructose (so it's suitable for diabetics too). There's also 6 mg protein and 5 calories per teaspoon (although heaven knows how anyone managed to catch it on that teaspoon). The pH value is 7.2 (good for your skin!). By the way, the greatest medically proven shooting range is 29.7 centimeters (11.7 inches), although a cursory glance at any porn movie would suggest that's exceedingly modest.

▶ With an average of 11000 jizz orgies throughout the course of his life, each man will shoot between 30 and 50 liters of sperm, so three men could fill a bathtub. The 100 million men per day who have sex on this planet could easily fill a swimming pool. Ready for a dip?

Taste

I rather doubt that you'll immediately like the taste of your own sperm, but this would be a pretty useless manual if I didn't know how to positively influence the flavor. You can consume highly concentrated fruit extracts, eat sweet fruits, or drink fruit juices. Tropical fruits are especially useful here: pineapple, mango, papaya. They not only taste good—their enzymes keep you healthy, and taken in conjunction with your own body's sperm you're well on the way to immortality. Smoking and eating meat can turn this elixir of life into a bitter medicine, and I'm reluctant to even mention asparagus. Sperm with a soupçon of cabbage might not taste that fantastic either.

Eating your own sperm: a question of good taste.

From lust to a sense of wellbeing

▼ The art of pleasurable anticipation

Okay. Up until now, buffing the banana has merely been hot and varied, and hopefully a little entertaining too. Let's now move on to how you can progress from sheer horniness to a sense of wellbeing. One thing that'll help you here is to stop focusing exclusively on your dick, and include the whole of your body instead. Another is to make the arousal phase more interesting, and/or prolong it by using some very simple methods, because this enhances your anticipation of the grand finale and is also the best prerequisite for becoming multiorgasmic—I'll also go on to talk about the tears of joy you'll eventually shed. Multiorgasmic? Don't worry, we'll get around to discussing that later. Why should you prolong the arousal phase? As I wrote in the introduction, taboos have prevented most of us from ever learning to enjoy masturbation, and instead we've just been intent on getting it over as quickly and quietly as possible so that no-one notices anything. If you're wanting to change something radical about your jerking off routine, you need to take a little time.

The ever-popular bathtub wank: Relaxing, but unfortunately forms rubbery lumps in your chest hair.

▼ Craniosacral pump

If you repeatedly tense your ass cheeks while you're jerking off, you'll activate the craniosacral pump and ensure that the energy which accumulates in your pelvis while rubbing is pumped up via the spinal column. This way the energy won't be discharged so quickly. Not least of all, it's a good basic exercise for the Taoist sex secrets I'll get around to discussing later on.

▼ Breathing

Breathing is so taken for granted that we often forget the extent to which it can affect our experience. Experiment with it! When you're having solo sex, hold your breath repeatedly for several seconds. Or breathe more deeply than usual. Breathe quickly and then really slowly again. Force your breath out, or pant superficially. Draw your breath down into the tips of your toes, and then breathe again using only your chest.

Experts use breathing to direct energies. To put it simply: If you notice while jacking how energy increasingly gathers in your abdomen, you can spread it throughout your body with the help of your breath, thereby delaying ejaculation or even preventing it. You'll not merely experience a genital orgasm, but a whole body orgasm too.

▼ Noises

It naturally affects your breathing if you grunt, groan and whimper: You're forced to breathe more deeply. This in itself is a source of greater pleasure, and many men think it sounds hot—unlike the phony "Oh yeah baby, lick that hole!" But something else really crucial happens if you allow noises to emerge: Your body starts to vibrate. Just place your lower arm to your lips and hum/buzz into it with your mouth open. You'll notice that your entire body vibrates. I haven't yet worked out why vibrators are hot, but the sales figures suggest they are. So allow yourself to make a noise! Grunt! Drool!

Say rude words (perhaps not when you're in the office restroom, although...). Not least of all, it's ideal preparation for hot groaning à deux. But don't give it any thought; just let it emerge of its own volition, and that way it'll remain natural and genuine.

▼ The whole caboodle

Of course it's incredible fun to play around with your bits—so much so that many men forget their body consists of more than just their cock. There's pleasure to be found in other parts or areas of the body. How does that wonderful poem by Eichendorff go?

"There's a song that slumbers in all things
As they dream on and on
And the world begins to sing
If only you say the magic word"

Um, was that too literary for you? No, you got the message: You just need to find the right sort of touch, the right stimulus, and even your kneecap will produce a marvelous song. Here are a few magic words that are guaranteed to work—assuming a little patience and sensitivity.

Abracadabr...ass

Biology teachers (the evil bastards) have systematically been engaged in a conspiracy whereby they never mention all the fabulous nerve endings that surround the asshole (which is why it feels very sensual to touch). Enough is enough! Freedom for assholes! Of course many men only think of fucking when it comes to assholes, but you don't always have to immediately go for it—if you know what I mean. You needn't drill down deep if you're squeamish about shit, although you'll be missing out on something. This section deals with quick and universally applicable methods, so let's stay in front of the Great Gate of Happiness, moisten our (middle) finger and use it to massage the dark side of the moon.

The more daring among you might enjoy this technique: Get na-ked, put a bit of lube on the middle finger of your non-jerking hand, and massage your asshole until your cock is erect. Grasp it with the hold of your choice, then move your pelvis as if you were fucking your hand. Every time you move backward, your slippery finger will penetrate your ass and your foreskin (if present) will also pull back with each forward movement. In this way you stimulate your

A hold for the cognoscenti: playing with your asshole.

cock and ass alternately, and your entire lower abdomen becomes energized. 'Fucking yourself' is also perfectly acceptable in the office restroom.

Sensual pleasure

But I'm getting caught up again in pre-orgiastic imaginings. Before I go into the pleasures presented by other parts of the body, I ought to say that you can not only stroke yourself, but also knead, scratch, pinch, rub, tickle, squash, hold and touch.

Balls

Balls like to be swung, which is something we've learnt from government officials who do nothing else the whole day long, and—and top of it all—get paid for that. Beside fondling them, you can also rub them, tug at them a little, tap them, or even squeeze them. One amusing variant: Find some soft cord or a long strip of material (e.g. the belt of your kimono); tie a loop in the middle and place it around your ball sack, then attach the two free ends to your ankles. This way you can alter the tug on your balls when jerking off by simply moving your legs. There are some more macho practices later on in this section.

Perineum

You should become especially familiar with the area between your balls and ass, because we'll need it later on when we're talking about delaying imminent ejaculation. Until then, let's turn to the sensual stroking and massaging of this area. With many men, it gets quite moist during arousal and has a wonderful odor of earthy, tropical air. If you're keen on it, you can sniff your slippery fingers (the more senses you incorporate into your love games, the more multiorgasmic the finale will be). But don't forget the massage. If you apply pressure here it will be transferred to the prostate, the male G-spot, and that can't ever be massaged enough.

Nipples

As far as nipples are concerned, many men are initially just as shy as they are about playing with their ass. It's seen as feminine, or not masculine at least. How dumb. Why shouldn't men be allowed to have as much fun as women? Why were these things provided with such sensitive nerve endings if you weren't supposed to enjoy them? So cast the myths aside and try it out!

A delicate turn of the buttons helps to fine-tune arousal.

It's definitely not enough to just stroke them once as an experiment, because you won't immediately get a rock-hard stiffy. Areas of the body that have never been activated or have been neglected for ages have to be discovered at your leisure. I can still remember the first time I was asked to minister to some male nipples. "What's the point of that?" I thought. But because he got off on it like a rocket, I subsequently played around with my own—after all, I wanted to have fun too. But: absolutely nothing doing. Quite the opposite—it even turned me off. Only when another playmate devoted a great deal of attention to them did they begin to awaken from their Sleeping Beauty slumber. In the meantime my nipples have been transformed into on/off buttons (the left one more than the right, in case we ever meet). If playing with dry fingers doesn't do it for you, try using a little spit, or lube is a real treat for them too.

Feet

Let's devote a few lines to those parts of the body we're constantly trampling upon. In truth I'm not exactly a foot fetishist, yet I can report that the sensual stimulation of the soles of your feet can trigger a rich sense of wellbeing. Licking your own toes is unfortunately something we'll have to leave to contortionists, but there's little to prevent you from stroking the soles of your feet, investigating the gaps between your toes, or (drool) fondling your ankles. It's a canny idea to use a bit of lube, but don't forget to wipe it off before you attempt to stand up.

Well, there are plenty of other areas which deserve our attention and can work a little magic. You can send shivers throughout your body if you gently brush the insides of your knees, and by simultaneously pampering the side of your body you'll find yourself enjoying a truly special type of sensual pleasure. Oh, and please don't forget your armpits ... and have I already mentioned the neck?

Do you fantasize about construction workers? If so, why not sniff your armpits?

The whole caboodle

Ass
Balls
Perineum
Nipples
Feet

Insides of knees
Side of body
Armpits
Neck/throat

▼ Techniques that will help you tense or relax

Practice this technique lying on your back—it's easiest that way. Completely relax, then start to wank slowly and gently, but enough to get aroused and maintain this arousal. Every time you sense that you're tensing a muscle, deliberately let it go again and focus on your arousal. It takes a while, but things will eventually come to the boil. And now for the exciting moment: Stay relaxed when you cum. Simply maintain your jerking speed and yet stay relaxed all over your body. If you can manage that you'll experience a totally different kind of orgasm. Alternatively you can try the opposite: Jack off perfectly normally, and shortly before you cum tense all your muscles as firmly as possible, including the ones in your face. If you let go again after you've cum, you'll be inundated by a surge of heat which will make you see stars.

▼ Delaying

You've learnt how to increase arousal by playing with your body, so I'm now going to explain how to prolong this state and thereby produce maximum pleasure. Orgasm and ejaculation aren't independent beings which mysteriously creep up on you when you're least expecting it, but physical reactions you can influence and control.

The Million Dollar Spot

This technique has been handed down from the Tantra. It prevents you from cumming by interrupting the ejaculation reflex.

I wouldn't be much of an author if I didn't like telling stories, so here goes. Legend says that a Tantric Master called Lu the Immortal discovered this spot which, if it's pressed hard enough at the right time, allows orgasm yet prevents ejaculation. His disciples were sworn to secrecy, but of course the world eventually got to hear of it. Over a hundred years ago a fabulously wealthy American decided to learn the secret.

Most teachers he encountered made only vague allusions to it. One posed a puzzle with the following metaphor: "As long as the cobra is coiled up, it is quiet and poised. But if it rears up to strike, it becomes vulnerable." Try working that out if you can. If not before, this will all become to you once you've read the section on Taoism.

The American naturally understood nothing, and got very annoyed: "Goddammit, isn't there just some spot I can push?" An old man who had been sitting in the corner of the room all this time smiled at him: "If you give me a million dollars, I'll show it to you."

Ever since then there's been a big temple at this place, and Master Lu's secret has spread all over the world. Some people used it as a method of contraception before the Pill became widespread, and under the alias of *coitus saxonus* it enjoyed a certain vogue—naturally it's far too unreliable, but we needn't concern ourselves with that.

In order to find the spot, touch your perineum (the area between your scrotum and asshole). Roughly halfway between them you'll discover an indentation, although it can also be closer to the scrotum or ass—every man is different. If you press firmly onto this point just before orgasm you will, so to speak, trap the ejaculation. Ideally you will experience orgasm without cumming, which means your cock remains hard. If you press just a little bit too late, the sperm shoots into your bladder, and is rinsed out when you next take a leak. If you only press once your cock is already twitching, your cum will still fly into your face and it'll merely hurt a little. The same applies if you don't press hard enough.

Tugging your nuts

Lots of men stop themselves from ejaculating by tugging on their nuts, while pulling like this makes other men really horny. Others can experience both at the same time: They get hornier, but can't ejaculate. Perfect. Try it!

The tennis ball

Incorrigible rapid spurters can simply sit on a tennis ball (or similar) which is placed under their perineum when they jerk. This constant pinching ought to delay ejaculation for quite a while.

The squeeze technique

Particularly suitable when you're jacking off: you just need to squeeze your glans firmly—preferably where the glans meets the shaft—and hey, the arousal is halted.

Spreading your legs

The same applies to spreading your legs. Devotees of S&M use this knowledge to deliberately prevent their slaves from ejaculating. It's quite a challenge to shoot your load if you're tied to a St. Andrew's cross, but that doesn't apply to everyone either.

Ice cubes

This technique is supposedly used by Arabs; at least that's what the movie *Overboard* starring Goldie Hawn tells us. Maintain arousal until just before orgasm, then dip your hands up to your wrists in a bucket of iced water (a champagne cooler would be doing it in style). If that's not available, there's another way of cooling your ardor (from the Tantra too): Form a 'U' with your tongue. If you now breathe in, the air will feel much colder. Give it a try now! It will cool your arousal without strangling it.

You won't cum as fast if you spread your legs – how hot is that?

Breathing

Not least of all, you can accelerate or postpone orgasm by deliberately controlling your respiratory rate. When you're approaching your climax, your heart begins to race, heat rises to your head, and your breath becomes faster and shallower. But you can delay orgasm if you consciously reduce your respiratory rate and breathe deeply and calmly instead of quickly and superficially.

Noises

Just as instinctive grunting and making noises can spice up the sex act, the avoidance of grunting, groaning and growling can slow the process down.

Thoughts

Learn to control your thoughts. It's said that thinking about ejaculation helps to induce it, so if you think, "Shit, I'm about to cum!" it's already too late. So don't think about it! And don't think any negative thoughts either—they distract you from the eroticism of the moment.

Delay methods

The Million Dollar Spot	Ice cubes
Tugging your nuts	Breathing
The tennis ball	Noises
The squeeze technique	Thoughts
Spreading your legs	

▼ How to prevent tendon sheath inflammation

I expect you're wondering what on earth that might mean. According to an English study, most men aren't accustomed to playing with themselves for more than five minutes, so they rapidly develop problems with their wrist as soon as they start to take masturbation more seriously—which is precisely what I am encouraging you to do in this section. Apart from the fact you'll delight any doctor when you initiate them into the causes of your discomfort, you might have a job that's hard to perform with stiff wrists (believe me, I know what I'm talking about). So what's the solution?

▶ **Work on your technique:** Don't just use your wrist to jack off, but deploy the strength that lies within your shoulders. You've clearly been overdoing things if they get stiff too.

▶ **Make sure your arm stays relaxed when you're jacking.** Rub really slowly, and as you're doing so press gently from the shoulder right down to your wrist. Which muscles are tense? And which are unnecessarily tense? Which can you relax and still be able to jack off?

▶ **If aches and pains have already developed,** the only remedy is cold poultices, anti-inflammatory creams, and rest. One more thing about this English study: It revealed that the average man only strokes 59 times before he cums. Gay men (54 strokes) are even quicker than straight men (62). See: ▶ www.lovehoney.co.uk/shootout

▼ Cock rings

So-called cock rings (which you place around the base of your penis) can help to delay ejaculation. They also make your cock thicker, the veins on it stand out, and your glans becomes redder and more engorged.

Sure, you can also push drapery rings from the DIY store over it, but consider this: Drapery rings are intended for drapery rods, which couldn't care less if welding seams give them the occasional

A small, unobtrusive ring has a major impact.

scratch. However, your cocktail sausage might not be so happy about this.

There are different types of cock ring, so let's start with the rigid ones. This is how you get into rings made of metal, hard rubber, or neoprene: First one ball, then the other, and finally push your flaccid prick through. And that's the first problem. If you already have a stiffy you won't be able to get rings like that over it. Second problem: You have to measure so that you buy the right size. Place a shoelace tightly around the base of your cock (behind your ball sack!), measure the length and then divide by pi (3.14 recurring). A rough guide: The majority of customers need 4 centimeters, but don't hesitate to email me if you end up with more than 7 centimeters. If it works out at more than 10 centimeters, you've obviously miscalculated. If the base of your cock isn't as round as the metal ring you'd like to buy, you'd be better off choosing one made of a softer material.

You can also get items (mainly made of leather) which you strap to your cock with the aid of press studs. Advantage: They can be attached when you're already erect, and you can also get them off again if (perhaps as a result of taking Viagra) you're suffering from a permanent hard-on. Disadvantage: If you're unlucky, the press studs are positioned in such a way that the ring is either too tight or too loose. Alternative: Velcro.

You can also get flexible versions made of silicone (my favorites).They look pretty damn tight, but are so stretchable that they'll fit any cock. You can buy transparent ones so your partner won't immediately realize you're wearing one. They don't trigger airport metal detectors either. Disadvantage: They can get caught up in your pubes.

If you want to try out first whether a cock ring will increase your enjoyment, tie the soft belt of your bathrobe around your knob—but with a bow, so you can undo it as soon as it hurts.

▼ Condoms

Jacking off while wearing a condom provides some erotic diversity: Lots of men find the tightness, the crackling, the look, the smell, and of course the feeling of the material itself erotic (just like a rubber fetish). Furthermore, it's a wonderful way of preparing for sex with another guy; after all, condoms can come in very useful there too. The various brands can differ greatly, not only in terms of colors and flavors, but sizes too (the European Union norm states that all condoms are 17 centimeters long, but the diameter can vary between 4.4 and 5.6 centimeters). You can also get different shapes (there are straight ones, but tapered ones too), and this has some not inconsiderable consequences: If you're wearing a poorly fitting condom, sex can be less exciting, you can lose it (inside the other person), or your erection vanishes.

"I think condoms are crap," says Ramon, and thereby misses the opportunity of his life.

You can avoid embarrassment of this sort by playing with different types of condom at your leisure, in order to find the ones that are ideal for you. 'Extra strong,' 'Strong,' or 'HT' are roughly twice as thick as the regular ones. Many people think this promises increased protection from all sorts of pathogens. The stronger material is more noticeable, and you either love that or hate it. People who are allergic to latex can switch to polyurethane condoms.

Experiment with dry and moist condoms in order to recognize the difference. If you fail to find one that fits nicely, you're not alone. Surveys suggest that many men have problems with EU-standard condoms. There's a bigger choice in the US, although you might not want to be caught smuggling them into Europe. Incredible, but true: You'd be prosecuted.

If you practice at home, you'll also learn how to put them on at lightning speed, which is essential if you're so horny that your cock feels an urgent need to disappear into your partner's ass. However, you should also use this time on your own to learn how to make a show out of putting on a condom, so you can incorporate it into sex as an additional erotic element.

How to put a condom on

▶ Check the use-by date (irrelevant if you're jacking off, but it's best to get used to looking for these things)
▶ Tear open the pack (don't use teeth or sharp objects)
▶ Pull your foreskin right back (if you have one)
▶ Place the condom on your glans, with the lip of the condom on the outside (so it rolls down properly)
▶ Roll it down the shaft as far as it will go
▶ Don't despair if skin or hair get caught up in it, or if the condom rolls inward in places. With patience and a little spit ...

▼ Masturbators

96.3% of men apparently do it with their hand(s), but how do the rest achieve happiness? (Scratches head) Well, for example, with...

Melons, pumpkins, etc.

Ripe melons in particular have a wonderfully slippery consistency, although the skin is very tough. Once you've made a hole to fit the dimensions of your cock, the opening will remain this size. This means the massage effect isn't all that great, certainly no comparison with the tightness of a hungry sphincter. Nevertheless, you might not always have one on hand. And, um ... you can adjust the temperature of the melon. If you want to fuck something cool on hot days, put the thing in the refrigerator beforehand. Of course you can warm it up too, but all fruit and vegetables contain one helluva lot of liquid. This means it'll quickly get hot, especially in the microwave, and this is something you'll feel more from the inside than the outside! I can predict gloom and despondency (not to mention third degree burns) if you insert your weenie into a boiling hot pumpkin. So it's best to put your finger in first and test it. Your tongue would be even better.

Liver (vegetarians should skip this section)

Liver can be a splendid option too. Choose a nice thick piece at the meat counter, cut a slit into it, and off you go. When you've finished, it might be advisable to throw it away rather than put it back in the refrigerator because one of your buddies might get the munchies and suddenly fancy some *fegato alla Veneziana*. And wouldn't that be offal ...

Water wings

If you're young enough, you might even have some water wings lying around at home. Dads can use the ones belonging to their children—but only when they're not at home. And don't leave any trace of sperm, because Mom might get annoyed and the children could be emotionally scarred for life. It would be better to buy your own. Inflate them, apply lube (oils and grease are okay because they aren't made of latex), then insert your cock. One disadvantage compared to professional devices (see below): Water wings have very sharp seams, so you'll rapidly get some nasty cuts if you go at it hammer and tongs.

Miss Softie, WaterWoman, WaterHunk

Professional manufacturers offer a superior range of equipment; for example, the quaintly named 'disposable pussy.' Plastic (polyurethane) bags are welded together in a particular way and then filled with water; they're supposed to feel like a pussy because of their silky surface, which is thanks to the corresponding lube. You can get a version with two water chambers, which is meant to feel like a pussy, and one with three, which is supposed to resemble an ass—the manufacturer must be straight. The 'WaterHunk' is only available in shocking pink, which is why the name 'WaterQueen' would suit it better. The light-blue 'WaterWoman' is almost transparent, so it's easier to see your cock rubbing back and forth in it—and cumming.

Contrary to appearances, these things are extremely tear-resistant; one survived a fall from a chair without bursting. However, you probably ought to take it gently to begin with, and the noise when you're thrusting takes some getting used to as well. You'll be sorely disappointed if you rely on manipulating your cock to cum (by pressing, massaging or tickling). One major plus: These items are totally unobtrusive and can even be accommodated in your wash bag, so you'll never be alone when you're traveling (on business). All the same, they're not exactly cheap because you're only supposed to use them once.

▶ www.softie4u.com
▶ www.waterwoman.com

Fleshlight

Let's now move on to what is (according to the manufacturer's advertising) "the world's most popular sex toy for men." The *Fleshlight* looks like a flashlight. You unscrew the cap at the front, and (depending on what you've ordered) a mouth, butthole, pussy, or slit appears, into which you can duly push your trouser snake. Lurking behind this you will find (once again, depending on your order) a smooth, tight or super-tight cylinder, possibly with ribs or dimples. At the end of the Fleshlight is another cap. If you keep it closed, it creates a vacuum when you're fucking (suction effect), which is an additional stimulus. In order to wash it, you can simply remove the 'insert' from the hard sleeve and rinse it out. Dry it, powder it, screw it up, and pop it back on the shelf.

Apart from the design, one positive thing that strikes you about these things is that the material doesn't stink like the usual stuff that's supposed to feel similar to skin, so hopefully it isn't full of toxic chemicals. The feeling you get from this gel-like 'real feel superskin' is sensational—the consistency is a bit like soft gummy bears, and it's almost as moist as a real mucous membrane (although lashings of lube are required). Nevertheless, a real man is of course somewhat different. One advantage that shouldn't be ignored is the hard and very light casing, because it can be wedged underneath

your mattress or into the upholstery of your favorite armchair, thereby allowing novices to practice hands-free fucking while experts can pass the time of day until the next cute ass comes along.

As with all these stick-your-dick-in devices, the disadvantage is that you can't directly touch your cock (or whatever) while you're cumming, and it's just stuck in there, which is all the more disagreeable if you have to put up with ribs, dimples and tightness. Cocks over 20 cm (8 inches) long have to unscrew the exit unless they enjoy bumping against the cap or don't want to be fully inserted. There's always a danger with any stretchable material that it will lose its tightness over time, and then it's heading for the trash can. Okay, 80 dollars or thereabouts isn't the end of the world—just think how many beers you'd need to drink before you get a guy out of his clothes, and then sex with him might actually be less exciting than using a *Fleshlight*.

The smooth inserts are naturally easier to clean, but the dimpled or ribbed ones make you hotter. Some forum users suggest you shouldn't use baby powder to care for them because that supposedly makes the material brittle.

▶ www.fleshlight.com

The Docker

This toy doesn't really belong here, because at best it's only suitable for solo sex if you're cut and would like to feel what it's like to jack off with a foreskin. This sleeve feels like a gummy bear that's been through a pasta machine, and is actually intended for twosomes. Insert cocks into either end until the glans meet, and then jack off as if it were just one cock. It's even better if each partner puts one hand around it, and both people more or less hold hands and wank. It's absolutely great if the two of you cum at the same time. More vigorous rubbing with bigger dicks is off the menu because the thing is only 12 cm long, so is it really worth the money (around $12)?

Masturbators

Melons, pumpkins, etc.	WaterHunk
Liver	Fleshlight
Water wings	The Docker
Miss Softie, WaterWoman,	... and plenty of lube

▼ What to look out for when buying masturbators

▶ Your cock should be the right size for the masturbator.

▶ Soft parts will stretch, and will become less tight if you use them energetically and/or over a longer period.

▶ It should be visually appealing to hold the thing in your hand and/or look at it, otherwise there's only a slim chance it'll give you pleasure once it's on your cock.

▶ Remember you'll eventually have to clean the thing in some way or other. The harder that is, the less inclined you'll be to do it.

▶ The dirtier the toy, the greater the risk that all sorts of germs will be lurking on it. The more germs there are on the toy, the more likely it is you'll end up with a sore willy.

▶ How handy is the device? Weight, size, length?

▶ The noises it makes while you're playing with it aren't irrelevant either. Any object that's filled with water will make a gurgling sound, and you have to like that.

▶ Materials with a soft surface are full of softening agents. The sniff test will reveal all: If it stinks, it probably contains hormone-like substances that might be harmful to health. As an enlightened customer, you ought to read up about the different materials. However, they aren't the focus of this manual, so here's a website that in my opinion contains everything you need to know: www.holisticwisdom.com/sex-toy-materials-glossary.htm

▼ Vibrators

When I was toying with the idea of writing about vibrators, it initially made me grimace. My experiences with them go back quite a while. I was around 15 years old when my best buddy at the time and I ordered a surprise package from a major erotic supplies retailer. It contained a doll (of a female), which surprisingly I wasn't interested in, a vibrator, and a novel from the early twentieth century about the life of a Viennese hooker. In short: The book was the best thing about the package. But because I was forever stumbling upon the 'Bird of Joy' (see below) during my research on the internet, I gave it a try and, Jiminy Cricket, I discovered the delights afforded by vibration.

WaterStimo

The same company that manufactures the fuckable plastic bags (see 'WaterHunk' above) sells a vibrator called the WaterStimo which can be attached to the WaterHunk with Velcro. This device makes a dreadful racket, especially when combined with water-filled bags. However, the water transmits the vibration splendidly, and you can feel it all over your cock. 10 programs (from 'bzz' to 'rr-rr-rr') guarantee very pleasurable stimulation, and with a bit of practice it's perfectly capable of bringing you to orgasm. I'd be lying if I didn't admit that I naturally clamped the thing around my cock and balls too, and that on its own is worth the purchase price (around $35). However, you should only insert it if it's wrapped in a condom.

PVibe

The English company PVibe is attempting to conquer the highly competitive toy market with a fancy device which is shaped like a small 'H' (it can also be used as a pendant). You attach it to your dick with the help of an elastic ring, and it starts to vibrate. The vibrator is extremely quiet, and the vibration very intense because it's directly transferred to your prick. The advantage is that you can put it on and still have two hands free to jerk off, so you can either leaf through a back number of *Readers' Digest* or massage your tits. If you feel it lacks a potentiometer (a rather apt word in this context) to regulate the strength of the vibration, don't forget that this device was developed for fucking. The vibration is gently transferred from the cock to the mouth, ass, or pussy, and changes automatically as it goes deeper. Depending on whether you want it in steel, silver, or gold plate, the device will cost you from around $140 to $300, but it's a luxury toy which shouldn't be compared with the cheap plastic devices that might be found in Mom's bedside drawer.

▶ For more information, go to www.pvibe.com.

Bird of Joy

This should be contrasted with the 'Bird of Joy,' manufactured by a German company called Nobra which is run by a married couple near Hannover. The bird envelopes the cock with its wings and then uses its beak to massage the frenulum (the band of tissue between the glans and the shaft). Nevertheless, in order to enjoy this avian pecking of your pecker, the latter needs to be at least 6 inches long, although maybe you can agree on something shorter with the manufacturers. The noise when running is minimal. You could even conceal its use from your sleeping partner—if the bird didn't make the whole bed shake. And last but not least, the beak is also suitable for body orifices or just hollow areas—there are no limits to your imagination. As if that didn't provide enough reasons to buy one, it's available in 12 colors and is totally odorless, so almost certainly not toxic. In order to really get you going, the speed of its vibration can be controlled very accurately. If you still prefer to slam the salami in the bathtub, you'll be reassured to discover that the bird is waterproof—although the electricity supply definitely isn't. It can also be remotely controlled via a computer, which is tantamount to true cybersex because anyone can download the software.

One disadvantage, in my opinion, is that the device itself is rounded in places. Most cocks are also rounded underneath as a result of the urethra, so that makes it rather unstable and not very

well supported, so you might have to hold it in place with your hand. Since the other hand is needed to control the speed (I'd recommend a constant up and down to begin with), you really need a third hand to devote itself to your tits. Solution? The 'Nobracontrol,' with whose help you can work out and save programs on your computer in advance. Alternatively, you can wait until Nobra launches the version with two motors, where your cock is sandwiched between them. So-called banana dicks, i.e. ones that bend upward (approx. 25% of men have ones like that) will presumably not be adequately massaged by the bird's beak, but I can only assume that. Around $180 is pretty steep, but up until now I've only ever encountered satisfied customers in chatrooms. And just imagine: Never have to rub again! It does it all on its own.

▶ www.nobra.de

Now, you might be wondering why I even bothered to list the PVibe if the 'bird' appears to do so much more. This is because the PVibe offers one crucial advantage: It was made for fucking. And I can only confirm that suckers, especially deep-throaters, are particularly enthusiastic about it.

Vacuum cleaners

Since austerity is now the order of the day, I'd also like to devote a few lines to alternative methods which can supposedly be enjoyed with the aid of (household) appliances—and we're mainly talking about vacuum cleaners here. I've experimented with this, but the nozzles on my two vacuum cleaners have an interior diameter of 3 and 3.5 cm respectively. How are you supposed to cram an 'erect member' into this? You can insert it while it's still flaccid and apply suction until it's stiff (which is actually very amusing, but only until you reach the point where it exceeds a thickness of 3 cm). However, the motor will quickly get hot if you do, which makes it a very expensive pleasure. I can well imagine it's fabulous to ejaculate in the air flow, although I've never tried it because I find it hard to accept that dried sperm improves a room's air quality.

The idea of using a milking machine is similarly silly. Just take a look and see how long it takes to rinse these devices out after milking. It isn't worth forming an alliance with a farmer's boy simply to get your weenie sucked off once—unless he uses his lips.

Vibrators

_WaterStimo   _Pvibe
_PowerStroker   _Bird of Joy

▼ **What to look out for when buying vibrators**

▶ Switch it on and feel the vibrations in your hand; it at least gives you an impression.

▶ However, you're constantly bombarded with pseudo-music in porn stores, which definitely serves to distract you from the clanging and clattering of cheap devices. This can certainly put you off once you're groaning away quietly at home, and it's virtually impossible to use it if your parents are in the next room.

▶ Consider that you somehow have to hold the thing in your hand. If it's too heavy you'll get a paralyzed arm, and if it's too light it won't transfer many vibrations.

▶ Not least of all, the crucial question is whether it'll fit your cock (shape, length, diameter, etc.) Asian devices may be cheaper and more accomplished, but they're mainly aimed at a clientele which, on average, is slightly less well-endowed.

▶ I may be a poor author (cue violins) and need to think about economizing, but I'd advise you to invest a few dollars more rather than resort to cheap devices. Experience demonstrates that you'll soon be forced to buy the better one anyway, so you end up paying double.

▼ Anal toys

Because I've already devoted an entire tome to anal play, I'd like to refer adepts to *Bend Over! The Complete Guide to Anal Sex*. For everyone else, I'll try to give you the bare essentials here.

Dildos...

... have some advantages over genuine cocks: You can control them yourself. You choose the shape, size and texture you prefer off the shelf, and it stays hard for as long as you like. One thing that all insertion techniques have in common is that you have to master the art of sphincter relaxation. The outer sphincter can be controlled by willpower, but the inner one does as it pleases. It opens voluntarily if it senses pressure from inside, because it thinks something needs to be expelled. However, once the cunning besieger has slipped inside the open gate he should devote particular attention to the prostate. This walnut-sized object sits approx. five centimeters above the anus, and richly deserves its reputation as the male G-spot; you can achieve anal orgasms by stimulating it. Not many people derive any pleasure from rummaging around up there as if they were kneading bread, but a delicate massage or even being prodded by a powerful in-out can sometimes be electrifying.

If you don't want a stranger's dick up your ass, and would instead like to exclusively restrict yourself to autoeroticism, you can build your own cock with the help of 'Clone-a-Willy.' This kit contains precise instructions and all the materials you require.

And for my next trick, ladies and gentlemen ...

Electric toys

It's not just monsters from Frankenstein's laboratory that like to be plugged into the mains from time to time. Professional electro-stimulators (not model railway transformers please) make you itch, tingle and throb.

Spanking

If you'd like to increase the intensity of your internal stimuli, you can spank your own ass. But beware! There's no skill involved in wild thrashing. Taps and gentle smacks that slowly get harder aren't just a form of sensual pleasure, but also increase the circulation in the anal area, which promises more intense orgasms.

Rino Tama...

... a.k.a. love balls/beads. This sex toy (originally developed for women) comprises two hollow metal or plastic spheres which are the size of table tennis balls. One is empty, the other full. They hang from a string and are inserted into your backside. They start to tickle and vibrate with each movement, thereby increasing your sense of pleasure.

Vibrators

Of course you can also get vibrators that perform very impressively at the tradesman's entrance. You can insert them as required and then have both hands free to juggle with various other parts of your body. Penis-like devices are intended to mimic being fucked: in/out with an added 'brrrrrr'—lovely! However, this once again means one hand is occupied with this. Alternatively you can get vibrating butt plugs (us gays have been such a blessing to the sex industry), and they're imaginatively known in straight stores as 'poop stoppers.' They have the fabulous advantage that you can wear them under your clothes, so if you get terribly bored during a meeting on Capitol Hill you can just switch it on (now you know why many politicians are always grinning.)

Cheap devices can be had for around $30. But beware, as already pointed out with cock vibrators, cheap isn't necessarily good, and it's rather unpleasant to have a battery explode on (in) you.

Perhaps I could refer connoisseurs of refined toys to the 'Cigar' by PVibe. As slim as a cigarillo (1.3 x 10 cm), it fits into all sorts of tight spots and will happily come to rest in your rectum. It isn't as quiet as its little brother 'PVibe,' and there's one thing I really don't like: The end is provided with a loop through which you can thread a string which will help you to retrieve it from the nether lands. A variety of things could get stuck to that, so you should always use it in a condom to avoid any nasty surprises. On sale at $139–$239.

Anal toys

_Dildos
_Electric toys

_Spanking
_Rino Tama
_Vibrators

▼ What to look out for when buying anal toys

▶ What goes in must come out again, so only insert things that have a base, handle or some kind of bulge on the end. String, cord, etc. can dissolve when it becomes damp.

▶ Beware of cheap goods: Welds/joints can injure you, overheated motors can burn you, and short circuits can lead to explosions.

▶ Don't buy very fragile toys. The contractions of your sphincter during orgasm are more violent than you might imagine.

▶ Bear in mind that these objects need to be washed too. The more indentations, openings and dimples they have, the yuckier it'll be to clean them.

▼ Care instructions

With any device or toy, you should pay attention to which lube the manufacturer recommends. Okay, it'll usually be something they make/sell themselves because that increases their profits, but on the other hand you can drastically shorten the life of your toys by using the wrong liquids (oil-based lubes ruin the surface of latex dildos). The same applies to cleaning: It's never advisable to put anything, even a dildo made of tough plastic, in the dishwasher or washing machine.

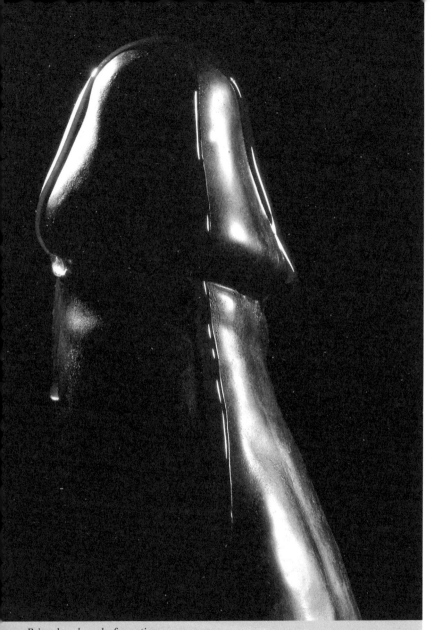

Primed and ready for action.

Where should I buy?

Naturally it's tempting to buy the stuff as cheaply as possible, and of course that's recommended by the countless spam emails that arrive on a daily basis. However, you'll soon be disappointed if the money's already been taken from your credit card but the toy is still at the warehouse, on a rusty container ship en route from China, or (more likely) merely a figment of some fraudster's imagination. Sure you can start litigation, but disreputable internet businesses are counting on their customers being too embarrassed to complain (would you fancy telling a lawyer that you'd ordered some jizz-covered socks but they never arrived?). Secondly, e-commerce is ideal if you're planning to make yourself scarce before any lawyers' letters drop into your mailbox. That's why I'd always buy in a store, simply because you can touch, examine, and even sniff the goods. Not least of all, it's a bit like burger advertising (in my opinion anyway): They look fresh and juicy on the billboard, but the minute I get my clutches on them the salad looks brown and limp, the bun tastes like cardboard, and the meat is as dry as a witch's tit.

▼ How do I store sex toys?

This might appear to be a stupid question, but in actual fact different materials aren't always compatible because they cause chemical reactions. Discoloration is perhaps the least of your problems, but it points to the fact that an aggressive process is underway. It makes sense to be slightly pessimistic in this context, because caution is preferable to having your life cut tragically short. So if you're planning to buy things which presumably aren't that healthy, store them in such a way that the different materials don't come into contact with one another.

▼ Jerk-off material

Heavens, I'd almost forgotten to write about jerk-off material! There's plenty of it, even though I reckon it's better to manage without, simply because you can become excessively dependent on it.

Porn movies

I'll only mention them since this is supposed to be a pretty exhaustive manual, because everyone knows they exist and what you're meant to do when you watch them. The advantage is that everything is pre-digested: The guys are provided for you and they show you how to do everything, so you simply need to play with yourself and you're good to go! Disadvantage: It isn't exactly easy to find the right movie. I personally am turned off by 95% of them simply because of all the dumb groaning, so I can best enjoy them by using the 'mute' switch. I think it's even dumber if they pull silly faces in order to look particularly masculine when they're having sex. That provokes the opposite reaction in me: I think they're idiotic rather than masculine, which is why I've taken to enjoying porn movies with the TV switched off, which is much harder than you might think. So I'd advise you to watch the movies before you buy, or even better: Just borrow them!

One-handed literature

Beware, this is an author talking here: I think written jerk-off material is preferable, simply because it leaves more scope for (and encourages) your own imagination. The argument that one hand is out of action because it has to hold the book is, in my opinion, of little consequence because I have to devote a lot more attention to watching a porn movie, attention which could otherwise be focused on my own body. In any case, you could buy one of those book holders you see advertised in magazines. The major disadvantage of reading is similar to that you find with movies: You first have to find something you think is erotic—for example, something published by Bruno Gmünder (of course!).

Inspirational: watching other men have sex.

Underwear catalogues and promotional photos

My generation discovered sex via underwear advertisements in mail order catalogues. Nowadays all sorts of models in fashion advertisements are suitable as jerk-off material, but I better not mention any brand names because I want to avoid product placement (unless they pay me for it).

Photos

Photos work even better, and you can download them from the internet. I'm not talking about commercial providers who charge money for this, but chat portals or websites where amateurs nowadays promote themselves like professionals (or do they maybe expect to be paid if you go on a date with them?). Slightly more expensive (yet not relying on the presence of a computer) are illustrated books which any gay bookshop will have on its shelves.

Your own imagination

Picture your dream partner and incorporate him so realistically into a sex scene that you believe it might actually happen. The greater the detail, the more exciting it'll be. What does he look like? Height, hair color, clothes? What characteristics does he have? Is he passionately aggressive or somewhat submissive, or both at the same time? What does he kiss like? What do his lips feel like? What does his mouth taste of? Is he cut? Does he produce precum? What are his balls like? How does his voice feel when you lay your ear on his chest? Which words does he frequently use? Does he have a pet name for you? What kind of noises does he make when he's having sex? Make him do everything you want from him; he's your creation, and you shouldn't have any inhibitions. Give yourself to him, or take him. Lick, bite, get him to spank your ass, tie him up. Only do what turns you on! Reinforce the experience by activating all your senses: smell, feel, listen. Have rubber, leather, gas masks, boots or underwear at the ready. Or maybe you could chew gum that tastes of 'him.' Lube could help you believe he's already cum on your chest or cock. Talk

Sometimes a photo in an advertisement is enough to spark your imagination.

to him. And of course—as ever: Give yourself time! This all works better if you have a wealth of personal experience, so roll up your sleeves and make sure you get out and about!

How to cum

An English study revealed that out of 1007 men who were surveyed, 111 used photos on their computer as jerk-off material, and 44 photos in magazines. 133 watched movies on DVD, 22 preferred video, and 209 movies on their PC. 285 preferred their own imagination, and 203 were inspired by a real person.

Parties/orgies, etc.

Some men prefer live action. There are plenty of places where men meet to jerk off together, and most of them aren't bothered if others stand next to them and have one off the wrist. Quite the opposite: It makes them even more excited. And surely, compared to sitting alone on the couch at home there's a slightly bigger chance that someone will give you a hand at a party. I'll be writing about the sight of men beating their meat as jerk-off material in Section 3 ('Time to get out of bed').

Jerk-off material

_Porn movies
_One-handed literature
_Erotic audiobooks
_Photos

_Underwear catalogues and promotional photos
_Your own imagination
_Parties/orgies, etc.

▼ Getting into the orgasm

Finally in this section, we should also devote some time to enhancing the experience of orgasm—bearing in mind that the techniques described above (which lead from lust to a sense of wellbeing) should in any case give you a more pronounced myoclonus (that's involuntary muscle twitching to you), otherwise you're doing something wrong.

Instead of the orgasm kind of creeping up on you unawares, you can well and truly strengthen it by 'getting into it.' The difference is then roughly similar to that between neighbors having a nice little chat over the garden fence and Meg Ryan's oft-cited restaurant orgasm in *When Harry Met Sally*. As soon as you're steering yourself toward the final orgasm, focus on the energy flow within your body, 'feel yourself into it,' notice the tingling, prickling and fidgeting, and simply reinforce it. Back it up with some noises too: "Oh, yeah, mmm, oooh, yes, yes … ." Bark, howl, or cry out! Follow the impulse to convulse your body, spread your toes, roll back and forth. Whatever happens, just take it to the nth degree!

Gasp for breath!

Obviously you'll be wondering why anyone would want to suffocate. What I mean, of course, is breathe more, and do it deeper, and faster! You know you breathe faster when you're aroused, that your heart races. This chain reaction also works in the opposite direction: Breathing influences your heart rate, and this accelerates the circulation.

So when you cum, just give it all you've got. Don't be satisfied with the usual 'cum and go.' Breathe quickly and deeply, fidget, shout out, snort, stamp your feet—and then congratulate yourself on such total commitment.

Now, where did I put that cum towel?

It's over

Once you've cum in this way you'll presumably collapse in total exhaustion. That's fine. But don't just snore away—sense this exhaustion too. Use the seconds and minutes in which you're lying amidst broken ornaments and an upturned bed to anchor this feeling in your body. The heaviness in your limbs, the warmth throughout your body, the harmony of your diverse and chaotically flickering energies, the emptiness in your head, and the unique peace and calm that underlies all of this. Remember the energy that this orgasm has set free. The more often you taste it like this, the easier you'll find it to access this state in everyday life without having to resort to your dick.

A good workman knows how to handle his equipment.

3. Time to get out of bed! Changing places

It's also hot to get yourself in the mood by masturbating in unusual surroundings or situations. I was recently cycling with my better half through the gloom of the Tiergarten (a huge park in downtown Berlin) when a completely naked man came toward us. Okay, he was wearing sneakers, but not a stitch of clothing ... and that was on the sidewalk next to a main road. We decided not to ask whether he'd just fertilized the trees with his seed.

Taboos can add spice to sex: In this case, the taboo of walking naked in public (streaking), but of course you don't have to take it that far. It's perfectly adequate to pump the python while you're sitting in an armchair and Dad is having a midday snooze on the couch, or to play with your noodle under the desk in school (I know I've already mentioned this five times, but it's one of the most exciting jerk-off experiences in my innocent and otherwise so mundane life). However, you shouldn't take it so far that you can no longer get it up without this thrill. Dependence of any kind is a limitation.

▼ In the bathtub

It's indisputable that it's great fun to whack off in the bathtub. Nevertheless, you'll subsequently have to cope with an accumulation of frog spawn if you can't manage to spurt the cum in a high arc so that it misses the water, or even swallow the whole load. And that's far from ideal, especially for hairy bears.

▼ In the shower

The alternative: in the shower. It's particularly enjoyable to make deliberate use of the stream of water to get aroused; what a wonderful feeling it is to get your cock massaged in this way! Aimed directly at the glans from below, you'll soon be suffused with a sense of wellbeing. Far be it from me to annoy those of you who are cut, but: If you're equipped with a foreskin, unscrew the shower head so the water emerges from the hose in a thick stream, and then push the head into your extended foreskin (you might want to squat for this). Adjust the water pressure until you've found the perfect level, and it won't be long before your dick is rock hard.

▼ Camping

This is the harmless alternative to open-air sex. You're outside, and yet hidden from prying eyes—so long as you don't have a light on, because the shadows are bound to betray you. All you need to do is keep your mouth shut and not shout out all sorts of filth, such as, "Sit on my face, I want to stick my tongue into your hot little asshole! Yes, you pig. Cum all over me. I want the whole lot!"

▼ Under the desk at school

You're probably bored stiff by now that I'm forever telling you how I jacked off under the desk at school, but you can see from that how thrilling it must have been—but only if you've completely mastered the 'Dead Man' technique. Getting caught and being shown up in front of your fellow students is only amusing if your ego is strong enough to be proud of this deed rather than ashamed of it.

▼ Under other types of desk

Um ... the paragraph about the desk at school was aimed at high school students. I wouldn't recommend it to teachers, even though I get shivers running down my spine whenever I think about how I caught our English teacher while he was giving us a dictation. He was stroking his engorged prick through his pants (a huge mother!), and I would have been more than willing to get on my knees in front of him. Homophobic boys—and schools are full of them—would have reported him, and things would have turned out very badly. But of course there are desks in open-plan offices too...

▼ In the elevator

Masturbation is particularly amusing here because you need to be pretty damn quick. A 100-story skyscraper isn't an alternative either, because their elevators are really fast. And that would get rid of any erection I might have.

▼ In the tanning booth

What a pleasure it is to be naked, with the breeze from the fan blowing onto your overheated skin. It's part of the 'how to jerk off in a tanning booth' etiquette that you should clear up thoroughly after yourself and not just hope that nobody notices the spunk stains.

▼ In the changing room at a department store

Okay, you've grasped the principle by now: Sex while other people are present is a blast because of the risk of being caught. There can be no objection to it so long as nothing and nobody comes to any harm. So don't jack off into clothes you haven't yet paid for or frighten the saleswoman with your gigantic erection, and don't leave any mess! Not least of all, make sure you don't become dependent on being stimulated by dangers of this sort, so that it'll still be fun at home once you've closed the drapes and poured yourself a glass of wine.

▼ In the subway

As already mentioned, many people get a particular kick from being watched when they're having sex, but anyone who enjoys doing it in front of elderly ladies should be warned that they probably won't appreciate it. I'd also like to remind you that a group of drunken tough guys might get on at the next stop, so if you happen to have your hand in your zipper you might get the sort of kick you'd never imagined possible in your wildest dreams.

▼ Mud, glorious mud

Why is it so much fun to wallow in mud? It must be a throwback to our ancestors, although I'm not sure they actually wallowed in mud. We aren't descended from pigs, are we? Although ... never mind. A date was recently telling me about a lake outside Berlin which is visited every day in summer by a young man. He arrives on his bike, undresses, and folds his clothes neatly over the handlebar so they won't get dirty. He then wallows in the mud until he gets a hard-on, ejaculates in front of the astonished onlookers, swims for a while to get himself clean, gets dressed again, and calmly cycles home. Only in Berlin! However, you shouldn't emulate a man from Cornwall, England who has a cow manure fetish; he was jailed for 2 years in 2011 for repeatedly masturbating in a farmer's muck spreader. The court was told: "He was naked apart from one sock, and was covered in cow excrement and mud. There were tissues littered around him."

▼ Lakes, rivers and oceans

The lakes, rivers and oceans of this world can't be entirely free of sperm; the water massages you wonderfully while you're swimming, and if you go skinny-dipping your weenie will be nicely stretched out and your balls will be floating in the current. That can be quite arousing. If you then happen to see other men walking along the shore and their physical features correspond to your typical prey, you can definitely get a hard-on. Why not grab a cock?

This is another area where the 'Dead Man' technique comes in handy, which makes me think of another story: I was once at a spa complex, and I immediately noticed there were only men sitting in the jacuzzi. Dyed, bleached, conspicuous beards, what can I say? They might as well have shouted, "Hi, I'm gay!" It was definitely slightly bizarre that they were all staring so strangely in front of them. So I studied the lot of them and soon realized they weren't terribly adept at the 'Dead Man' technique. After all, they were sitting in a spa in broad daylight and jerking one another off. There are a great many things that could be said about this, but I'll restrict myself to: You can not only masturbate in lakes and oceans, but in all sorts of public bathing establishments. Do I approve? Well, just imagine you're swimming along merrily somewhere and a string of sperm comes floating toward you ...

Back to our origins: sex in water.

▼ In the open air

You could fantasize for pages as to why it's such fun to jack off al fresco. The feeling of being at one with nature, the sky above your head, the universe, Native Americans, shamans, smoke signals, and the gods looking down on you ... not least of all, the wind nibbling at your swollen glans and the leaves whispering naughty words into your ears. To be honest, is it ultimately (yet again) about the thrill of getting caught?

▼ On the internet

For quite a few years now, the internet has been the preferred place to get/have sex. Cybersex simultaneously combines several advantages: You get into contact with other men you'd never meet in ordinary life–people in far-off countries, politicians, closet queens who never go to bars, and even the occasional author–quite apart from evil lesbians who pretend to be guys in order to annoy us gays. Besides that, you don't need to buy anyone a drink, and you don't have to listen to really dreadful life stories before moving on to something more enjoyable. By contrast, you're allowed (nay, obliged) to respond to questions about your height, age, dick size and sexual preferences in an imaginative way that will show you in a kindly light. You can even send photos that aren't even remotely connected to you (not mine though, if you don't mind). Every partner will thank you for transforming yourself into his dream man. Not least of all, screen to screen contact is an excellent way of having safer sex, although you can get addicted.

By the way, we're only talking about cybersex here, since there's a whole new set of rules if you're planning to meet your partner live.

Something that's problematic with cybersex is coordination between jerking off and typing. Constantly sitting in front of a screen doesn't exactly increase your ability to enter into fulfilling relationships with other people, although one advantage (albeit rather nasty) is that there's no other place where you can so quickly get rid of the other person—just click your mouse. That's rarely a nice thing to do, but sometimes it's totally justified (not to mention necessary), for example if the person you're talking to does things that haven't been agreed (I'm reluctant to describe my experiences in any detail because they'd make you gag). On the other hand, the men you're chatting to can switch you off as well. Since some people are less sensitive and compassionate than us two paragons of virtue, that can also hurt from time to time—just grin and bear it like a man.

Another disadvantage of cybersex (and in my humble opinion it's the greatest loss, although tastes differ) is that you have to manage without lots of human stimuli: the smell, the feeling of a beard on your stomach, the soft lips of an expert kisser, the taste of his asshole, and perhaps most importantly of all, the warmth of another body.

Cybersex

A great deal has already been written about how to find good chat/cybersex portals, set up a profile, and extol your charms, so we won't detain ourselves with that here. It's more important to know how to make cybersex hot, since that appears to be a mystery to many people.

It's common to send "Hi" or "How you doin'?," which admittedly is a start, but (a) it doesn't offer the other guy much to be getting on with and (b) it doesn't give you any certainty about your chances.

A direct question is preferable: "Hi, would you like to chat?"—or more direct: "I like you." Or immediately flirt with him: "I'd really like to push my fat cock between those lips," "I got a hard-on the minute I saw your asshole" or "Wow, what a cock! I wouldn't mind having that between my legs." Naturally it makes sense to study his profile beforehand so you're aware of his preferences. If he takes the bait, you can continue in precisely the same vein. Write down your desires and fantasies. Ask him about his. Above all, always stay very matter-of-fact. Metaphors can be misunderstood, and the widespread "Please read between the lines, because I don't dare write what I want" will in 95% of cases be a complete flop—and not as pleasurable as you'd hoped. In order to get some inspiration for computer sex, it's helpful to study (written) pornography.

Special tip: Enter straight chatrooms using a suitable female pseudonym, such as Pussy, Sandy or Dominatrix, and go on the prowl. If you research the basics beforehand, such as the ideal 36/24/36 figure, you won't be short of new (heterosexual) buddies. Studying profiles is also advisable if you want to cater for the other person's preferences, although they're very limited in the straight world. 80% want a blow job (yawn). You don't know how to do it properly? Read *Blow Me! The Complete Guide to Oral Sex!*

No caption required.

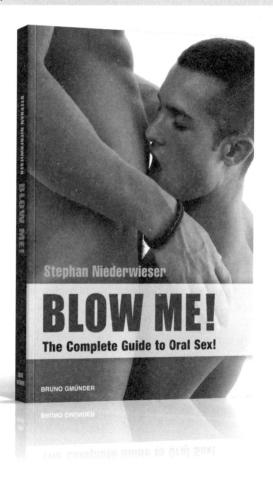

Netiquette

Whatever your fantasies, you ought to respect a few rules. They're a bit like a code of honor for people who chat on the internet—and unfortunately not everyone sticks to them:

▶ Be friendly! The person you're talking to is also online to have fun. Misunderstandings can be sorted out in a nice way.

▶ If you send pictures of another person, bear in mind that the person you're talking to might one day bump into the guy on 'your' photo—although this is unlikely if he's a nomadic yak herder living on the plains of Outer Mongolia.

▶ If you pretend to be a woman, a transvestite or any other kind of person, don't out yourself at the end. Leave your partner thinking he's just had sex with the horniest person in the world.

▶ It's a virtual world. Don't fall in love with your sex partner, because he's probably cheating just like you.

▶ Be careful if he asks whether you'd like to get to know him; the world looks pretty damn rosy after you've cum. Say instead: "Let's talk about it again tomorrow."

▶ If you discover inconsistencies in the facts he provides you with, don't immediately bad-mouth him. It's just a game.

▶ Everyone has the right to be respected. Defend yourself against anything that exceeds your boundaries. Insults and humiliation are hurtful. If you encounter someone who makes anti-gay comments, report them to the webmaster. Every surfer gets an IP number when they go onto the net, and that can be traced back.

▶ Naturally the reverse is true too—your chats can also be traced ...

▶ Say "thank you" at the end. It costs nothing, and it might make the other person happy.

With a webcam

The virtual world becomes a bit more real if you acquire a camera (webcam). Instead of just writing about what you're doing (jacking off, twirling your nipples, inserting a dildo, pumping your cock, making a cup of tea), you can show the other guy what you're up to. Modern technology even allows you to hear his voice at the same time, although the speech quality depends on your connection. The rest is almost as if it were live, although there's no mutual touching. Inventors are constantly fiddling around and trying to find ways of making virtual sex a possibility; this is then known as 'teledildonics.' Whole body suits have turned out to be useless (quite apart from the cost, this requires a counterpart who possesses some way of controlling it), but people are constantly offering dildos or masturbators that can supposedly be remotely controlled via the internet and USB. I'm only familiar with the 'Bird of Joy' (see above), although I'm obliged to refer to the manufacturer's instructions because I've never tried it out.

Besides a computer, cam and possibly a microphone, webcam sex requires a program that connects you with other people:

▶ icQ ('I seek you') at www.icq.com
▶ Windows Live Messenger
▶ Yahoo! Messenger at www.messenger.yahoo.com
▶ Skype at www.skype.com

Once you've hooked up with a guy, it's all fairly self-explanatory.

▼ On the phone

The aural version: Lie on the couch and give free rein to your imagination.

Inexpensive: Have phone sex with someone you've already had sex with. This has many advantages: You're familiar with his body and he's familiar with yours, you know his preferences and vice versa. Moreover, the whole thing comes across as pretty damn honest because of course it might actually be happening. "I'd like to give you a blow job now, just like I did recently. Do you remember when I pulled your pants down on the balcony ..." But of course you can also do this with people you've 'met' in a chatroom. You've made one another horny via the internet, so you give them a call. However, switching media in this way (from the screen to the phone, i.e. from the eye to the ear) isn't always positive. I was recently chatting with a horny Canadian whose website showed him promoting his bulging assets in nice tight uniforms. I found him really hot, but then I heard his voice on the phone. I have nothing against men with squeaky voices; it's just that it can be difficult if, when you were chatting on the computer, you imagined a different voice to go with this body, with this intellect that could dream up such filthy sex fantasies. That was what it was like on this occasion. We ultimately ended up discussing the political situation facing gay men in North America: interesting, but not quite what I'd expected.

So let's go back to phone sex with people you know. Many men (at least many I've tried it with) don't have the chutzpah for this, but why? Surely you already know one another inside out, you've heard the other guy groaning, and you've seen the kind of dumb face he makes when he cums. So why not have phone sex?

The voice, groaning, and hot language can be stimulating if you have phone sex

Just give it a try! What can happen? If the other guy isn't interested, hang up and do it yourself, because of course you're an expert by now!

If you opt to pay for services of this kind (most gay magazines are funded via these advertisements), be aware in advance of the charges and the phone connection you're planning to use. It can cost you your job if you do it in the office, and you might be risking your neighbor's friendship if you use his phone while you're watering his plants.

▼ (Gay) saunas

Many people naturally find it incredibly arousing to see naked men. Gay saunas have the advantage that most men who go there are generously willing to share their orgasm with others. Theoretically this ought to lead to greater openness, although it generally doesn't. But that's enough philosophy for now.

▼ In the shower #2

Were you afraid I'd forget your favorite location, namely showers in public buildings? Did you think those hungry gazes in gyms and swimming pools had escaped my notice? Of course not. Ostentatious jerking off is widespread, particularly in countries that have a more inhibited approach to gay sex (Hungary, Turkey, Greece ...). Just mince past the showers, get a juicy partner in your sights, shower opposite one another and liberally apply soap your genitals; nobody could possibly take exception to the fact they get bigger. On top of it all, ejaculating sperm is almost undetectable in front of white-tiled walls. Unfortunately.

▼ Porn cinemas

Since these cinemas are exclusively frequented by men wanting to toss off, it's irrelevant whether you opt for a gay or straight cin-

What should I do with the sperm?

... you might interject. Everyone knows it leaves annoying stains on your satin bed sheets, and for that reason shouldn't be landing there in the first place. Nevertheless, it's a common mistake to believe that a mouth would be a preferable receptacle—unless it's your own sperm.

And the argument that it's good to swallow sperm so you can finally get a hot meal into your stomach isn't terribly convincing either; after all, burgers are available from a variety of retail outlets.

The assumption that you can let your own sperm dissolve on your tongue and then play a game of tonsil hockey with another guy isn't much better—but that's probably obvious.

It's certain that another guy's sperm on your unbroken skin can't do much harm (so long as you aren't allergic to sperm), so don't be afraid of getting wet. Your nipples will enjoy this slippery treat, and your chest and stomach won't mind it either. However, even if you like watching other men cum, sperm in your eye isn't safe (and it really hurts). What about getting him to cum onto your glans so you can use his sperm as lube? It sounds tempting, and I can assure you it feels awesome. I'd rate it as borderline in terms of the risks of STD transmission.

ema. Your gaze will in any case be directed not at the screen, but at the big fat cocks to your left and right and—beware!—behind you.

However, owners of straight cinemas occasionally patrol with flashlights so as to satisfy health and safety regulations of some sort, but don't worry if you happen to be bent over the back row in order to get a better fuck, because they won't bother you. After all, they need the money. You should just be careful with your clothes, because the back row is rarely free of stains ...

The risk of infection

People say there's much less likelihood of a plane crashing than being killed in an automobile accident, but what good is that if you're involved in one of those rare plane crashes? On the other hand, does this mean you shouldn't fly anymore?

Jerking off with another guy (or simply jerking him off) is pretty safe when it comes to being infected with pathogens of any kind. However, it's very tempting to suck someone off once you see their juicy fat cock, so I'll tell you a story. I recently spent some time with people and we were discussing Viagra. One of them claimed that what has now become a party drug was partly responsible for the increasing rate of new HIV infections. The rest of us didn't understand what he meant, so we asked him to go into greater detail. He explained that the pills not only mean that people who previously couldn't get it up can now enjoy an erection, but that men who are definitely still capable of getting a hard-on don't immediately go flaccid after they've cum. The logical consequence isn't very surprising, albeit rather frightening: The Viagra-enhanced cock stays stiff even if it has already ejaculated, so if you then suck on it you'll be treated to a generous portion of sperm that has remained in the urethra. Voilà. A survey that was conducted in San Francisco between 1996 and 1999 suggested that 6.6% of new infections could be traced back to oral sex. There's still a need for more information about this, so I'd refer you at this point to some reputable websites:

▶ www.aidsmap.com
▶ www.managingdesire.org/GaySexWithoutRegret.html
▶ www.avert.org/oral-sex.htm

▼ Darkrooms

Darkrooms are dimly lit corners, rooms or cellars in gay bars, porn stores or cinemas where men gather to have sex with each other. However, they're often wanting more than just a wank. Generally speaking, the level of hygiene in these places isn't beyond reproach, so there's a relatively big risk that you'll fall victim to all sorts of nasty bugs (and not just pickpockets). I know we're only talking about jacking off here, but even if you nobly resist all temptation and stick to hand jobs there will always be men who think it's horny to put their finger in your mouth. But do you know where it's been? So if you ask me, I'd merely say there are bound to be places where you can jerk off and not have so much to worry about.

▼ Sex parties

Lots of men enjoy going to sex parties, not to fool around with other men but to watch them having sex (or be watched in turn). After all, it's silly to always do it on your own. Big cities offer plenty of events where there's something to be seen: Bars often arrange themed evenings, but there are quite a few private parties too. If the gay listings magazines don't announce them, just rummage through profiles in chatrooms, and it won't hurt to ask local sex shop owners either. If no-one has gone to the trouble of organizing a sex party, seize the initiative yourself because people who always just moan are rather unattractive.

Jack-off parties

Since we're dealing with group activities here, I'd like to mention jack-off parties, which are sadly slightly out of fashion these days. They were hugely popular in the mid-1980s, simply because they offered an opportunity to have sex without any risk of infection. However, the introduction of successful combination therapies has meant that demand for them has slumped, and an awesome forum—

joint masturbation in groups—has bitten the dust. I think JO parties are great, because in addition to satisfying your lust they represent an ideal opportunity to learn from one another how to achieve greater pleasure, without (as at other sex parties) being distracted by men in gas masks and uniforms indulging in fisting contests or piss-drinking championships.

You can find some great advice about planning and organizing parties like this if you go to ▶ www.letsmasturbate.com/party. It's a bit like Tupperware, but without that awkward feeling that you really ought to buy a salad spinner.

Bukkake

While we're on the topic of competitions, deliberately spraying spunk onto other guys is called bukkake, which might initially suggest an obscure martial art or possibly Japanese flower arranging. The origins of this sexual practice date back to the 1980s, although the gay scene only adopted it in the mid-1990s. However, it doesn't merely entail jerking off onto someone, because the ritual involved and its aesthetic aspects are also important. There are a number of different versions: 'Painting the eyebrows' involves ejaculating along the eyebrows to the middle of the face so that the sperm drips over the eyes, while the 'bukkake cornhole' means you fill the ears of someone who's kneeling down. With the 'nasal spray,' you firstly aim into one nostril and then the other, and push the protein-rich juice into the sinuses—almost like advanced 'jerking onto a cookie,' and totally unsafe.

Groups can compete against one another in a kind of race. The team whose members (chortle!) cum first is the winner. Another option is a relay race where team members are only allowed to cum consecutively, and the order in which they do so is fixed in advance.

▼ Tea rooms

In Britain you could safely take your maiden aunt to a tea room for scones, clotted cream, and a nice pot of Earl Grey, but in the US this term describes a public restroom that's used for sex. I can't really explain why some of these places are favored for this purpose, but tea rooms are still very popular. Maybe it's because communal jerking off is rapidly and sometimes very unobtrusively accomplished in such locations; for example, straight Dads can also try their luck. Just go in, hold your dick over the piss trough, and wait until someone joins you. You'll soon notice if he's interested: Either he'll piss or he won't. Or he'll gawp at your cock. Or he'll offer you his (erect) member. Or he'll immediately jack off like crazy. Or precum instead of piss will drip from his prick (this happened to me in Vienna, in the shadow of St. Stephen's Cathedral). It's highly unlikely that he'll hand you a gilt-edged written invitation, so seize the opportunity while it presents itself! But don't forget! Cops go to public restrooms too, as George Michael discovered to his chagrin.

It's really offensive to overstep the bounds of common decency and jerk off in front of children (or anyone else who disapproves). I'm not going to question the law here, but simply point out that the courts might take a very dim view of this, even if you personally think it's dumb and boringly conventional.

▼ Parks

No park is small enough to escape the nocturnal goings-on of consenting gay adults. Communal jerk-offs under the stars are healthy. What's the procedure? Go for a walk, look up into the sky with a bored expression, whistle a tune, and watch. Is there someone sitting all alone on a bench? Is someone lurking in the bushes? Yikes! Move cautiously toward him. What happens next? If he runs away in panic, you should consider buying a new outfit. If he walks purposefully in front of you without hurrying, he's wanting to entice you to somewhere quiet where he can play around with you, show you

The dynamic of unsafe sex

Years ago, during my annual prostate check-up, my urologist encouraged me to get HIV tested again. I replied that this test always stressed me out terribly. The doctor wisely replied: "Come on, take the test! If you're certain you're negative, you'll practice safer sex."

I naturally rejected this statement as gazing into a crystal ball, but later on when I was all alone in my quiet little room it gnawed away at me. And you know what? I think he's right. After each test, my willingness to take risks was reduced to zero. But as soon as the first mishap occurred (sperm that landed in my eye in the heat of battle, a cock that started to produce precum when I was sucking it...) I didn't take it quite as seriously the next time – as if something in me was assuming: "Well, nothing happened the last time anyway." But of course you don't realize you're possibly being infected, so the last time should never be compared with this time. It's totally idiotic to think that way.

I'm in no way wanting to advocate testing, I'm simply wanting to draw your attention to the dynamic involved. If you engage in unsafe sex on one occasion, it's very likely that you'll be more willing to take a risk the next time, so it's better to not even go there. Don't think that 'just once can't do any harm.'

his stamp collection, or mug you the minute you're out of earshot. The moral of this tale is: Never carry important documents or large amounts of cash with you if you're planning to engage in this sort of activity, although it might be a good idea to have your name written on a piece of paper so that the police will find it easier to identify your corpse later on.

Many a nice surprise awaits you in a gay hotel.

▼ Freeway rest areas

Yes, sweetie, nothing is sacrosanct if you're a horny man wanting sex, and straights are no exception here. The major disadvantage of this location is that it assumes you have access to a roadworthy vehicle, and I'm not talking about a three-wheeler.

Okay, so on the one hand there are the restrooms, but we've already discussed them. Maybe I should mention here that it's worth deciphering the graffiti, not merely for its inherent entertainment value ...

> Here I sit all broken hearted
> Tried to shit, but only farted
> Then one day I took a chance
> Tried to fart, and shit my pants

... but because it might actually feature something interesting, such as:

'14 August, 8 p.m., in the red truck behind the restroom' (although possibly not with such fastidious punctuation).

Furthermore, rest areas frequented by gay men always have bushes or little woods you can sneak off to. Has it ever struck you that some cars are parked for ages even though there's nobody around? This is seldom because they're trying to spot some rare migratory bird, although it's probable that the drivers would welcome a shag.

Moreover, nowhere else will you encounter such a high concentration of truck drivers who've just woken up. When they crawl (still half asleep) from their bunks in the morning they mostly still have a semi-rigid cock (a.k.a. morning glory or the dawn horn). If you're there and ready to sacrifice yourself (possibly behind a tree so they can only see your stiffy), you'll be doing each other a favor.

Sex in front of (and with) other people

If you're wondering how you're supposed to manage that (getting out your willy so that others can watch), just re-read the interview with Jack van Dean at the beginning of this book.

Finally, there's the option of pleasuring drivers who are waiting in their cars. You can sometimes recognize their willingness to be serviced by the fact they're sitting in their car with their zipper open, showing off their magnificent erection. Okay, okay, it's not that often you'll get so lucky, but be honest: Why would a solitary man park at a rest area if he didn't have something dirty in mind?

▼ In the car

If communal jerk-off contests have whetted your appetite for more, you can of course give someone a 'lift' in your car. That immediately makes me think of the 1970s, when people still had sex in drive-in cinemas because that was the only place you could shoot your load. Those days may be long gone, but sex in cars is still exciting. On the one hand, a degree of creativity is required if you're going to get your

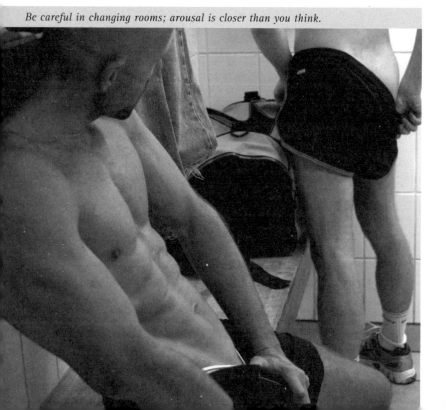

Be careful in changing rooms; arousal is closer than you think.

act together in such a restricted space. Secondly, you must of course possess the necessary muscle power to lift yourself or the other guy around and/or maintain an awkward position for long enough. Not least of all, there's the thrill of being discovered. However, don't attempt to drive while you're doing this. A couple in Munich who were multitasking in this way ended up in a canal, which understandably created quite a stir.

If it's a little too cramped for you in the car, why not try it on the car? Particularly just after you've switched off the engine, because the hood will still be lovely and warm. It's also arousing if you're caught at it and people gather outside the car while you're putting on a show. If you should experience such good fortune, show what you're learnt and place my books subtly (yet easily visible) behind the windshield, and don't be surprised if a trip to the car wash is called for once the show is over. Well, I think that's enough of all these stimuli. I'm sure you'll discover other locations and learn how to get into contact with other people there.

Places

_In the bathtub
_In the shower
_With a webcam
_Camping
_On the phone
_Under the desk at school
_In the (gay) sauna
_Under other types of desk
_In the shower #2
_In the elevator
_Porn cinemas
_In the changing room at a
  department store
_In the car

_In the tanning booth
_Darkrooms
_Sex parties
_In the subway
_Jack-off parties
_Mud, glorious mud
_Bukkake
_Lakes, rivers and oceans
_Tea rooms
_In the open air
_Parks
_On the internet
_Freeway rest areas
_Cybersex

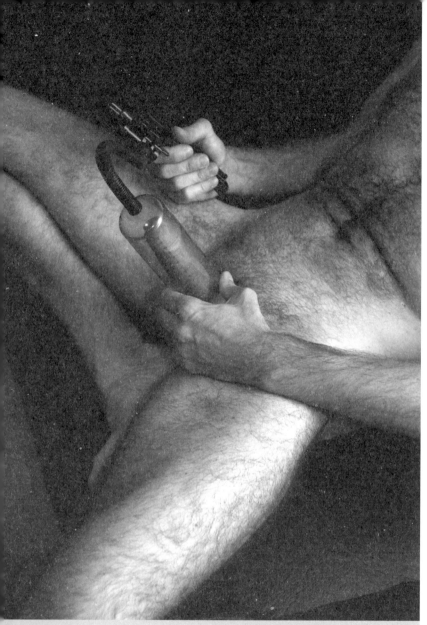

Tingling, heat, the feeling of heaviness – all this can be arousing...

4. Taking things to a different level: additional stimuli

It's said that approximately 10% of people in Western society rely on stronger stimuli when they're having sex (regardless of their sexual orientation). For that reason we'll now devote some time to stimuli so you'll know whether you belong to the vast majority or yet another minority.

▼ Shaving as sex

It may sound silly if you haven't tried it yet, but shaving is not only sexy in terms of its outcome (smooth skin, improved and better-groomed look, bigger impact), but also possesses a certain attraction in itself. You don't believe me? Try it!

Wet your cock and balls (warm water is sexier), apply plenty of shaving foam and massage it in. Aha, now you're beginning to understand, aren't you? Then use a normal wet razor (movable blades are better than rigid disposal razors) to slowly remove the hair from your cock and ball sack. Yummy, eh? And if your little friend sticks his head out while you're doing it, so much the better.

Beard trimmers and dry shavers are less appealing. The vibration may be erotic, but the skin down there is too sensitive for sharp blades. The risk of injury is high, and you won't enjoy it that much if you're not keen on the sight of blood.

▼ Creams and gels

For a while now there have been lubricants on the market that contain substances which can produce special sensations on your cock. Particular attention is paid here to simulated changes in temperature, so-called 'warming effects.' My cock sometimes perceives them to be cooling too, but that's no great surprise because it's rather idiosyncratic. This astonishing feeling of warmth above all makes you focus on your cock. 'Warming Lubricant' by JO Systems is a real treat: It keeps your prick warm for hours on end, and makes it smell like peppermint—and when you piss it smells like tea. There's no shortage of gimmicks either: 'Blow 'n Glow' by Eros doesn't only warm; the effect is made even more intense if you blow on it, which is easily done when you're jerking off (nice too if you're playing with another guy). By contrast, 'Frixion' with its additives derived from guarana, ginseng, yohimbe and the like aims at prolonging arousal. The manufacturer promotes it by calling it the 'natural alternative to Viagra.' You can also buy a lube (Mr. Ease) that contains muscle relaxants so it's easier (and pain-free) to get fucked, but that's not very helpful if you're jacking off unless you need to quickly hide your clandestine dildo.

If you don't fancy lube when you're playing, you can try the stimulation sprays sold by Excite. 'Stimul' and 'Volume' increase circulation, while the tingling cold/warm effect makes jerking off more sensitive. 'Volume' also tightens the skin, and the glans appears to swell (hence the name). The non-greasy gels are quickly absorbed, so there are no problems if you have to unexpectedly put on a condom ("Hey honey, why have you come home earlier today? I wasn't expecting you.") If you'd like to try this out first without investing too much money, you can experiment with essential oils: Cinnamon = hot, camphor = icy, cloves numb ... but please always ensure you only ever mix just one or two drops with lube in your hand, never directly onto your cock—that way you can't complain later on that I never warned you. In emergencies you can simply suck on a Fisherman's Friend (if he's not too busy mending his nets) and spit on your dick. Yippee! It's best to aim directly at your pee-hole; if it burns too much, you're obviously a weakling.

▼ Vacuum pumps

Having a bigger cock is a dream shared by around 70% of all men. Vacuum pumps can make this a reality, at least in moderation. However, they do a great deal more: They make you horny, and that's what we're aiming at here. The tissue fluid that's sucked into your cock and balls also makes your genitals heavy and spongy, and their sensitivity is increased.

Shave around the base of your cock so as to guarantee a better seal. You should warm your cock and balls (and preferably the entire abdomen) in order to increase circulation, then apply plenty of lube all over your cock as well as to the inside of the cylinder (it'll rub against the cylinder when it expands). Attach it and then suck out the air.

And this is what it can look like.

What to buy

▶ Buy a pump that suits your cock size. Remember that the corpi cavernosi (literally 'cave-like bodies' of erectile tissue) in the penis aren't balloons, and the bigger the cylinder, the more of a vacuum will need to be created.

▶ Cheap devices are less well finished. The consequence: less of a vacuum, seams, not very handy, and not very durable either.

▶ It's easier to operate them with one hand rather than two.

▶ A removable pump makes it easier to carry the cylinder.

▶ They can cost anything from $35 upward; elaborate machines can also set you back over $250. Computer-supported devices with penis stretchers cost far more than that.

▶ Sets that include a dildo and cock ring, etc. are much cheaper than buying each element separately.

▶ If you need it to enlarge a tiny pecker, talk to a good urologist; your health insurance might even agree to pay for it.

To begin with, the cock inflates to the size it normally only reaches just before orgasm. Then the piss-hole opens and the cock begins to tingle. The foreskin (if present) swells, as does the tissue at the base of the cock, which presses onto the prostate (G-spot), expels precum, and triggers the famous 'pumper's high.' If you create more of a vacuum, the flesh around your piss-hole will protrude and lymphatic fluid streams into the foreskin, thereby making it very thick.

It's important throughout to remain in a state of 50-70% arousal so that the necessary circulation is guaranteed. Porn magazines or DVDs can help here, and hot guys too. If you ask too much of your prick, you'll provoke ugly swellings and bruises. To begin with you should use the pump for no more than 30 minutes, and leave long gaps in between so that you can recover.

Jerking off after pumping may be incredibly hot, but it can damage the ultra-thin blood vessels in the erectile tissue, so you should jerk carefully (if at all) with a lotion that calms the skin (marigold or arnica ointment).

There's a website where you can see the result:
▶ www.tigerpumping.com

There's also a porn star called Mukhtar Safarov who's used the technique to good effect (google his name to find photographic evidence of this). However, it's not difficult to imagine the kind of damage this might eventually entail.

▼ Nipple play

I mentioned earlier on that nipples are wonderful 'pleasure switches' because they cause oxytocin to be produced when they're stimulated. And that makes you happy, which is evident from the beaming faces of breastfeeding mothers. The harder you play with them, the more hormones are released. So what are you waiting for?

You can also pump your nipples up, the cheapest way being to use disposable syringes. No, you can put your smelling salts away, we only need the plastic part of the syringe and certainly not the needle. You can get them from a friend who's a nurse, or via the internet.

Get ones that match the diameter of your areola (the area where red skin turns into white). Saw the front part of the syringe off and file it down so it's smooth and rounded. Then smear lube onto your tits (this provides a better seal), attach the syringe and pull out the plunger until the desired extension is achieved. You can comfortably walk around your apartment like that for ages. Your nipples will not only be quite a bit bigger afterwards, but incredibly sensitive—hooray!

Laundry pegs can be used to pinch your nipples, but they're hard to adjust so it's a good idea to get some professional nipple clips, preferably a pair that are attached to each other with a chain so you can simultaneously play with both nipples if you're on your own. Simply pinching them isn't going to be a great success.

For many men, piercings are only a source of pleasure to begin with, although later you can suspend weights from them or attach electro toys. I'll explain further on why some people pour wax over them. If merely stroking them doesn't turn you on enough and there aren't any teeth handy at the time, you can always rummage in your tool-box and find some pliers. Extremists attach castration rings (available from all good veterinary supplies stores).

▼ Assplay

Assplay is of course not restricted to the tedious in/out of dildos or vibrators, although it would be going beyond my intent to describe this in any detail here. For that reason, perhaps I could refer you to my manual entitled *Bend Over! The Complete Guide to Anal Sex.*

▼ The unusual and esoteric

Don't be worried if you're excited by things which at first glance have little to do with sex, for example materials such as shower curtains or velvet (or shoes, manhole covers, exhaust pipes, etc.). It's called 'having a fetish,' and it's only problematic if it hurts others or yourself, or if you can no longer get horny without using these things.

The same applies if you feel the need to do unusual things while jerking off, such as dress as a nurse or wear diapers. Now that's what I call kinky! Don't be ashamed of yourself, there's no reason why that should make you feel weird. Just enjoy what turns you on, but remember that if you're having sex with other people they might be put off by it. You shouldn't surprise anyone with your 'extreme' preferences, and certainly not expect them to get aroused too.

Who says that fetishes only add spice to party games?

Auto-erotic asphyxiation

One practice that has achieved a certain notoriety since it was featured on *Six Feet Under* is that of cutting off your air supply while you're tossing off, because a lack of oxygen reinforces the sense of orgasm. Some people become adept at hanging themselves from bedposts or gym equipment and then jerking off at the same time. The aftermath can be fatal in the literal sense of the word: You have to develop a technique whereby you're automatically no longer suspended once you've cum. The fact that this is by no means risk-free is sadly underlined by the premature deaths of many ordinary as well as famous people (supposedly 100 every year). And just consider how stupid you'll look when they find you.

That's why I shall refrain from giving you any instructions here, apart from: If you really must try it out, get throttled by someone you trust and who has experience of this. Otherwise: FORGET IT!

▼ CBT/CBP

CBT (cock & ball torture) is the general term for a whole range of cock and ball games which I'll subsume here under CBP (cock & ball play). CBP is very popular. What, you don't believe me? Well, you don't immediately have to imagine putting them on the barbecue. Although ...

Foreskin

Many men think it just gets in the way. In Europe, the foreskin is often dismissed as ugly, so people want to get rid of it. By contrast, cut Americans frequently think foreskins are awesome, and even fetishize them. Anyway, consider yourself lucky if you still have yours since many men whose foreskin has been completely removed can't jerk off anymore without using lube, so they even have to run around saunas with a tube in their hand.

You can also pull your foreskin back slightly harder or pull it apart when you're jacking off, so it hurts a bit. Some men tie it up so it swells when they cum (assuming you can manage to cum without wanking; see 'Persian-Indian style'). And if you're one of those fortunate guys who produce precum, you can insert a finger under your foreskin and smear the precum around, thereby stimulating your glans. Dry cocks can of course resort to lube.

Is the urethra just a one-way street for liquids?

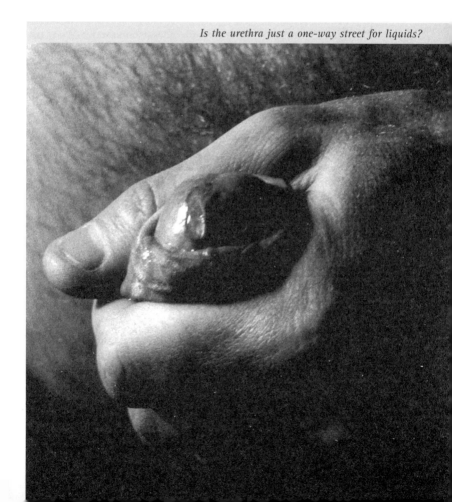

Spanking

As a warm-up, you can of course give your quivering cock a couple of taps/slaps on the side and see what it feels like. Or might it prefer to be pulled or twisted? If it relishes being punished in this way, you should up the ante by using mini-paddles (kind of fly swatters made of leather).

The urethra fuck

Contrary to ingrained prejudices, the urethra is by no means a one-way street, because inserting things into your cock can be one of the greatest sources of pleasure. But please be careful. Never use wood (splinters) or plastic (can break). Surgical dilators (stretchers) are rounded, slightly bent rods made of steel, and are available in various diameters. Start with a maximum of five millimeters, clean thoroughly with alcohol and/or a bactericide, apply lube, and ... insert slowly. Don't forget to apply more lube, because a 'dry' urethra can get irritated and subsequently bleed. It can also hurt and scar over, which can be hot (but not if your dick then has to be opened up and operated on). You should exercise particular caution if you push through to the bladder—if you actually get that far.

You can of course resort to a catheter as well: Rubber is warmer, more supple, the things are longer, and you can play piss control games. There's also this little pump to anchor the catheter, and you can inflate it before it ... ouch! Oh yes, and pissing burns quite a lot after a urethra fuck, which is hot too—at least for some people.

Urethra vibrators

This game can be taken to another level if you use a urethra vibrator (with a diameter of six millimeters); this small metal object makes your whole body tremble, and not just your cock. Guaranteed!

Diabolo

This is a metal rod that's anchored in the urethra via the hole in a Prince Albert piercing. A screw cap/ball on the end stops you from pissing, although it can be removed. And naturally you can attach an electrode to it (see 'Electro').

Pulling

In actual fact, balls aren't that incredibly sensitive. They know they're being squeezed or tugged, and you can feel this deep down in your stomach region; the remaining sensations are absorbed by the ball sack. One positive side effect of playing with your balls: You focus on the middle of your body.

Stroke your hand gently but purposefully along the scrotum. Squeeze your balls carefully and tug on them; depending on your position, you can also pull them backward between your legs. Perhaps you might even find it agreeable to twist the ball sack, but be very careful: Testicular torsion (twisting of the spermatic cord) cuts off the blood supply to the testicle and is extremely painful, and can even be life-threatening.

Hitting

You can gently hit your balls, possibly with a pencil or leather paddles, which these days are available as key fobs. You can of course use your hand too, and a fly swatter is suitable for bigger balls.

Baseball bat

Rubbing warms things up: Grip your ball sack as if it were the end of a baseball bat and rub it with your shirt tail or—if available—soft Velcro. Tickling (with feathers and the like) provides variety, and that's what's important.

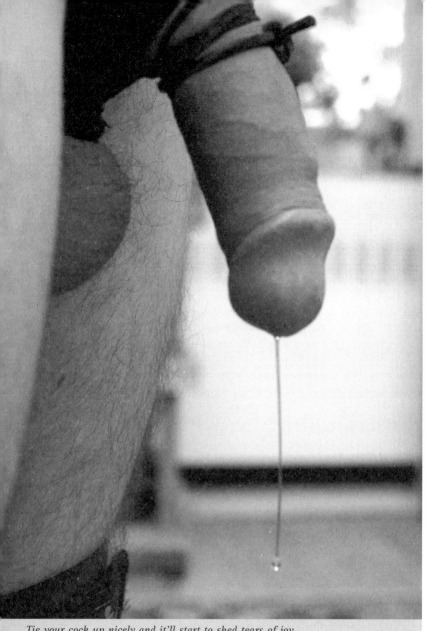

Tie your cock up nicely and it'll start to shed tears of joy.

Harness

You can attach a small harness which simultaneously serves as a cock ring and ball restrictor, and it's very easy to hang weights from it. If you don't have any handy, a boot will suffice. Some men clip laundry pegs onto their scrotum until it looks like a hedgehog. I'll be discussing wax and electricity-based games later on.

Pants hangers

You can use pants hangers to achieve more extreme pinching: either just the foreskin or the cock, or cock and balls together—it's pretty damn tight. This contraption can fortunately be found in almost any male household, and you can hang all sorts of things from it, such as weights or a sparkly Christmas tree decoration. Always make sure you haven't totally pinched off any important assets; if your genitals have already turned black or fall to the floor with a loud bump, you've waited too long.

Bondage

Bondage is the art of tying up individual parts of the body with rope, cord or cable. If you're a soloist you can enjoy the aesthetics and feeling (pressure, tightness, throbbing veins, bulging skin) if you tie up and restrict your cock, balls or nipples. It's not only the result, but the tying up itself that is hot. Beginners shouldn't play alone, but instead ask an experienced practitioner to keep an eye on them. Only use soft material with a diameter of at least five millimeters to start with, because anything thinner can damage nerves and blood vessels. Proceed slowly and above all carefully. Make sure you can quickly untie the knots again, because lots of things that were really hot before orgasm become unbearable afterwards, and the circulation rapidly decreases.

Once you've tied yourself up you can play with your genitals. Your bulging balls will be more sensitive to stroking, rubbing and gentle tapping, and they enjoy being sprayed with alcohol or pissed on.

Only when you've developed a feeling for this practice and gained some experience should you risk using thinner material or silver wire (très chic), and twist tight harnesses around your genitals.

▼ Enemas

From a medical perspective, you push liquids into the gut in order to clean it, or use its capacity for rapid absorption so that medication is more quickly accepted by the body. You hardly notice small amounts (suppositories), although you definitely can't ignore larger ones (more than one pint), and it's usually rather unpleasant, although that's precisely what might give you a kick. The gut contracts in order to expel the 'foreign body,' and you have to fight against that. Quite a few people really enjoy this tension, and it lends jerking off a particular *je ne sais quoi.*

There's no harm in trying it, but if you're wanting to take such anal delights further you should definitely learn how an enema and/or colonic irrigation works. The necessary apparatus can be bought in sex shops or sanitary supplies stores. Experts simply unscrew the shower head, although this can be dangerous: A sharp screw thread will tear your asshole to shreds, and if you can't control the water temperature there might be some unpleasant consequences. The charmingly unpredictable boilers in old buildings might be ideal for stimulating experiences in the shower, but not for sensitive rectums. Oh, and you'll need a toilet nearby once you've finished.

Really crafty people enrich the liquids they use in order to provoke specific effects, but don't forget the rapid absorption! Even a tiny shot of vodka will get you mortally drunk in a trice. Aspirin is nice and tingly, but it deadens any sense of pain. It's preferable to use mineral water (although not straight from the refrigerator). Poppers don't belong up there either, because they burn the mucous membranes.

▼ Hot wax

I used to play 'Dare' with my brother when I was a boy, dipping my finger in liquid wax and waiting until it formed a thick coating on my fingertip. The exciting thing about it was overcoming the pain. Do you dare? If so, you should beware of the following: Moderate heat is fun, but it's not very amusing if you end up with blisters, so keep your fingers away from beeswax because it burns hotter than ordinary stearin candles. It's also important to pay attention to the diameter: Thick candles quickly produce lots of liquid wax, while thin ones merely drip. Getting rid of tea lights in this way will burn your hands and ruin even the best nail varnish. And perhaps you're wanting to think about which color to use (hey, us queers have our reputation to think of), so naturally the candle ought to go with your bed linen.

It makes sense to place the candle within reach of the field of play. On the first occasion at least I would urgently advise you to previously apply oil to your skin; it protects you from burns and makes it easier to peel the stuff off afterwards. Hairy men will find it quite a chore to remove.

In order to get the hang of it, I'd recommend the non-hairy bits of your lower arms. It gets exciting if you move on to your chest, and the same definitely applies to your nipples. I'd only include the genitals in your repertoire once you've derived some pleasure from this 'foreplay,' because they're naturally a whole lot more sensitive.

By the way, you should never just pour it on, along the lines of 'now or never.' Playing with wax should be enjoyable, and your watchword should be 'drop by drop.' The height from which it's dripped is important too. The higher it is, the more of a psychological game it becomes (fear of pain); the lower it is, the more it becomes a sensual stimulus (actual pain).

▼ Watersports

'Golden shower' in contact ads or internet profiles doesn't mean the guy has expensive bathroom fittings: It's all about pissing. For some people, playing with their own urine increases their pleasure, while for others the very idea is disgusting. You should simply give it a try, if only to overcome embarrassment and the fear of urine (which is hygienically clean so long as you don't suffer from any kidney function disorders or urinary tract infections). The shower is the ideal place to eradicate any inhibitions. Start by aiming at your feet, legs or hands. If you lie down you can easily reach your stomach, and with a bit of pressure even your face. If you find that fun, ask your partner/another guy to shower you.

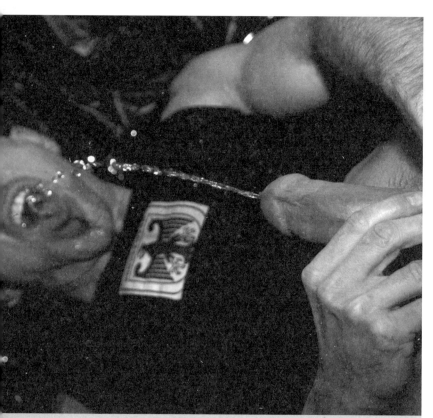

If there's no one to join in, you can get drunk on your own.

▼ NaCl (sodium chloride)

Strangely enough, a large number of reader emails that arrive on my screen these days ask what you can inject into your scrotum to make it nice and plump, just like they've seen on photos.

NaCl is 'physiological saline solution,' which means it approximately matches the osmolarity of blood plasma and can therefore be easily reabsorbed by the body. If you inject it into your scrotal sac it produces a tight, heavy sensation which temporarily gives you the impression you've got more between your legs than you actually have. And who can ever have enough of that? By 'temporarily' I mean that the solution is gradually reabsorbed by the body and the scrotum shrinks back to its normal size after a few hours (roughly one to two hours per 100 ml).

If you haven't ensured that everything's sterile, you're likely to get an infection which you'll be less happy to boast about. So: If you don't know what you're doing, better not play around. Even if you find an expert or you yourself are a doctor or a nurse, you shouldn't overdo it for the first couple of times. 500 ml is more than enough, and don't forget it'll take hours until you can fit into your tight 501s again.

It's a really stupid idea to inject silicone from the DIY store in the belief it's the same stuff women use to enlarge their breasts. I probably don't need to dwell on this, but I'm happy to respond to the question of whether you can use air instead of NaCl. The only problem is that air, unlike NaCl, isn't reabsorbed by the body, but instead will creep up into the abdominal cavity. It may be amusing to feel that a huge fart is brewing down there, but it's no joke if the air presses onto your heart and lungs because that leads to anxiety and shortness of breath. The only solution then will be to have an operation.

▼ Electro

There are stories going around that people are using model railway transformers for this purpose. It's not a good idea, because it can have some nasty consequences: burns, nerve damage, cardiac arrhythmia, or even death.

From a medical point of view, it's dangerous to attach electrodes above the heart, which importantly includes the head and the nipples too. It ought to be obvious that you mustn't do this in the bathtub, and people with pacemakers won't have much fun with either—at least not for long.

If you want to enjoy pricking, tingling and extreme pain, make sure you use professional devices that are made for this specific purpose. Go to your local sex shop and ask for advice. An experienced shop keeper will also be able to recommend nice accessories: Butt plugs with electrodes maybe, or the little wheels your mom used in order to mark out pieces of fabric. Clips can be attached to piercings, and you can then apply a little current ...

▼ Viagra (sildenafil citrate), Cialis (tadalafil) and Levitra (vardenafil)

All 'erection enhancers' block the enzyme PDE5 and thereby keep your stiffy rigid for several hours (Viagra 4, Cialis up to 72). However, they don't make you aroused, which is why they shouldn't be confused with aphrodisiacs. The possible side effects are not inconsiderable: Headaches, reddening of the face, inflammation of the mucous membranes, stomach ailments ... in rare cases it can even lead to priapism, a painful permanent erection which can cause lasting damage to the corpus cavernosum (erectile tissue). If used in conjunction with poppers, the blood pressure can fall to potentially fatal levels and lead to cardiac arrest. The long-term consequences cannot yet be predicted. As I've already mentioned, nobody yet knows whether your cock might not drop off at some point in the future if you take these substances regularly. That might worry a 60 year-old much less than someone who starts with these pills at age 25. However, one really dumb aspect is that most men may keep a hard-on after their first orgasm, but they no longer want sex.

Viagra, Cialis and Levitra are approved by the FDA in the United States, and are usually only available on prescription. However, many people don't buy them in a pharmacy because they're much cheaper via the internet (although you should be aware that some disreputable suppliers will try to sell you fake versions).

▼ Spanish fly ...

... is considered to be the oldest aphrodisiac in the world, and is produced from a beetle found in Southern Europe and North Africa. Cantharidin (its scientific name) is a powerful irritant which induces blisters. Its supposed aphrodisiac properties are the result of its irritant effect upon the body's genitourinary tract, and it can result in serious poisoning if ingested—even 4 mg is considered to be an overdose. The stuff you can buy in sex shops is generally harmless (and ineffective too), so don't waste your money.

▼ Drugs

Last but not least, self-love can be pepped up with all sorts of chemicals. I was originally planning to write a whole chapter about poppers, speed and crystal meth, but you know what? I think drugs suck—and not in a good way. I don't even like having sex with someone who's drunk, let alone with some hyped-up guy who's constantly experiencing something that's not actually happening. And have you ever kissed someone who sniffed poppers? It's like sucking on a text marker pen.

I have no intention of assuming the moral high ground here because I've tried everything myself, and I wouldn't necessarily discourage anyone from trying them. But do it in the company of people who like and respect you, and who will keep an eye on you so that you 'come down' safely again.

Okay, the argument that drugs make it easier to get infected with HIV doesn't hold much sway if you're doing it on your own. On the other hand, there's a considerable danger that you'll be willing to take other risks, such as auto-erotic asphyxiation. Lots of things seem fun and more exciting in altered states of consciousness (as opposed to sobriety), but you could fuck up your entire future. Bad ecstasy pills are one thing, but you won't be doing yourself any good if your heightened state of arousal makes you pour a bottle of poppers into your nose. Believe me, I know what I'm talking about; it has evidently burnt large parts of my brain, otherwise I wouldn't be writing one sex manual after another.

There are enough examples of gentlemen sticking their willy in food processors because they believed the ensuing pain to be fantastic. That may actually feel awesome if you're under the influence of drugs, but only once. And I ask you, what kind of an achievement is it to feel good with the help of drugs? Any moron can do that. It definitely won't further your personal development, and it won't increase your self-awareness either. On the contrary: That's been proven on many occasions.

▼ The Dead Man #2

You need this technique if you want to have sex when you're not alone, for example if your lover doesn't want sex with you but thinks that playing with yourself = cheating on him = bad = let's split up = your clothes are thrown out of the window.

Apart from learning how to jack off without any visible movement, you need to carry on breathing calmly and casually when you reach your climax, not to mention keep your mouth shut. A glance in the mirror will tell you whether you roll your eyes, squint and blink. Practice, practice, practice!

In order to conceal your orgasm from others who are present, you must also learn how to cum without ejaculating. This is also desirable in situations where sperm flying around wouldn't really be appreciated by everyone: Let's just say under the desk in an open-plan office (cleaning ladies are supposed to report this kind of outrage), in changing cubicles (simply because it's selfish and inconsiderate to make a mess), or in the swimming pool (sure, there are people who dive in with an unwashed ass or simply take a leak, but that by no means allows you to jerk in there). More about jizz-free cumming in the next section.

Learn some secret techniques—you can't always get your cock out of your pants.

▼ How to cum

In this case it's difficult to answer that question because I don't know what kind of games you've chosen to play, but you should bear two things in mind:

1. After orgasm, the glans at least (if not the entire cock) is extremely sensitive, so you should remove anything that's wrapped around your dick immediately while cumming (if not before), because hyper-sensitivity will otherwise put a mighty dampener on your orgasm.

2. As far as painful stimuli are concerned, if you've attached safety pins to your nipples and then suspended yourself from the curtain rail I'd advise you to free yourself before you cum because you can pretty much tolerate anything before orgasm, but during and after-wards that's highly unlikely to be the case.

How to ejaculate larger amounts

The simplest way of increasing the quantity is to bring yourself close to ejaculation several times before you actually cum. If you really want to provoke a mega-load, toss off for three days in a row until just before you reach a climax. More days are pointless, because the body then begins to secretly excrete excess spermatozoa without you realizing.

The secret of long-distance cumming

As I've already reported, the statistics suggest that most men are lucky to manage 12 inches, although I trust your experiences will support the fact that this is merely an average, and far from the whole truth. Some men are born with this ability (not right away, of course), but to a certain extent it can be controlled too: If you notice you're about to cum, pull your foreskin (if present) right back to the hilt so that your cock is tensed throughout its length. Point it straight and hold it in this position instead of swinging it through the air like a propeller. If you now squeeze your cock gently (not too firmly, otherwise the juice will go back into your bladder) you'll spray a lot further. It's also a question of posture/position, and you'll have to experiment to discover which one suits you best.

Jizz stains

Now all you need to know is how to get the jizz off your necktie. Hot water is undoubtedly the wrong method because it makes the protein coagulate and the cum is even more visible. It's better to soak the entire item of clothing in hand-warm water and a little detergent before putting it in the machine. Oh, but that hasn't solved the problem of how to clean your necktie, has it?

5. Cumming till they call 911: jacking off for experts

Jacking off is fun, helps you to develop a feeling for your body, improves your self-esteem, promotes sensuality, makes you healthier, improves your mood, gives you a sense of independence, and is extremely inexpensive. What if you could also make use of it to have more energy in everyday life, increase your ability to concentrate, make your cock harder, and counteract an enlarged prostate? Sounds a bit like winning the lottery, but your chances of success are far higher. It just requires a little training. Here's a little taster to warm you up ...

▼ **Persian-Indian style...**

... also known as 'hands-free' or 'goldfish sex.' However, the derivation of this term is a mystery to me, because 'Persian' actually means the man bathes his cock in warm oil before fucking (hot, but unfortunately not terribly safe because oil attacks latex condoms), and 'Indian' refers to sex where importance is attached to lots of different (complicated) positions, as in the Kama Sutra. However, Persian-Indian isn't a combination of the two, but merely the term for cumming without using your hand(s).

This 'technique' (if we can call it that) became famous thanks to *Sex and the City*, where a salesman gives Charlotte a pair of shoes with the stipulation that he can put them on for her. Well, and in doing so he creams his pants in front of her and the rest of the world.

Apparently 1 in 1250 men are able to ejaculate by merely focusing on sexual fantasies, a phenomenon recorded by the (slightly unreliable) sex researcher Dr. Alfred Kinsey in his famous report of 1948. This ought to convince the most skeptical of doubters that the head is truly the most important sex organ.

I can remember my first encounter with this phenomenon. I happened to be sitting on the face of a very hirsute beast, and while his tongue was massaging my appendix his cock suddenly reared up like a cowboy who's being thoroughly shaken by a bucking bronco, and thereupon threw a meter-long white lasso up in the air—and for goodness' sake, we'd only just started. Admittedly my butt is a pleasure to rim, but others have also managed to cum without rubbing or any assistance from me.

Well, I'm sure you'd now like to know how this can be practiced. To be honest, I haven't the faintest idea because it's never interested me up until now. As a child I was a master at the Florentine style, and I could imagine that's a good introduction to practicing Persian-Indian. The more you play with yourself and the more intensely you do it, the greater the likelihood that you'll also master this technique. I've found the opposite to be much more exciting: having orgasms without ejaculating. This is what I've occupied myself with, and I've discovered the following:

▼ Why it's dump to shoot your load

Sure it's splendid to spurt little white ribbons into the air and take delight in their acrobatics, not to mention the wonderful feeling that fresh, hot spunk leaves on your skin, but is that all there is? This moment of magic is duly followed by boring everyday life: Wipe it off, discard sopping wet paper towel, clean stains off the wall and ceiling ... and yet it could all be so much nicer, perhaps with another orgasm. Or two. Or ... okay, let's not get carried away.

The stupid thing about the ejaculation reflex is that it unleashes a chain of physical reactions. The 'refractory period' as it was described in the 1950s by the sex researchers Masters and Johnson includes: Pulse, blood pressure and breathing become normal again, and although the cock stays stiff for a while (depending on the length of the arousal and plateau phases) the erection is nonetheless blocked hormonally. The body is flooded with prolactin, which generally (apart from the odd exception) suppresses any desire for more sex. We become zonked, pooped, knackered. "Ultimately nature is less interested in our happiness than in a form of reproduction that is as economical as possible," says Harald Euler, a former professor of psychology at the University of Kassel and an expert on evolutionary theory. And if that's not enough to deter you from the guilty pleasure of ejaculating, just remember that the refractory period gets longer as you grow older.

Just imagine the cost savings if you could manage multiple orgasms: The demand for ecstasy pills would plummet, and Pfizer could donate its Viagra to the Vatican.

If you're now expecting a link to a pharmaceutical company, I'm afraid I'm going to disappoint you. You can't buy stamina. Sportsmen have to train regularly, long and hard to get themselves fit for championships, and the same applies to anyone who wants to experience orgasms without ejaculating and/or have harder, firmer erections. The solution is literally within your grasp.

What might sound like a pipe dream concocted by an author overdosing on poppers is one of the best-kept secrets in modern science. Just imagine if all those terrorists knew they were capable of multiple orgasms—we would undoubtedly be living in a better world. What I'm trying to say is: Learn it and promulgate it, so that people are happier!

▼ Recent research

The Belgian doctor Chris Goossens has discovered that soccer players' pulse rates increase faster if they've had sex the night before the game (naturally including the classic Western-world ejaculation). At the moment of maximum performance, for example when a forward is eye to eye with the goalkeeper, this factor can mean the difference between defeat and victory, concludes Goossens. And we know how important soccer results can be. So ejaculating not only shoots down the dream of hour-long orgasms, but also ruins the ability to concentrate the next day. Dumb, eh?

But how can you manage to cum without ejaculating? As early as the 1970s, the sex researchers William Hartman and Marilyn Fithian discovered how to do it. They studied the orgasms of 751 participants and established that 33 of them possessed the innate talent to cum several times. The most successful of them, John, managed no fewer than 16 climaxes within only 50 minutes, and by no means proved to be a one hit wonder. He reproduced this result for 25 weeks in a row without any decline in performance.

Naturally that sparked the doctors' curiosity. Their research led to the conclusion that all men are able (sooner or later) to suppress their ejaculation reflex and thereby experience a series of 'dry' orgasms.

▼ More (improved) orgasms

Step 1: Okay, I've tormented you for long enough. You want to know how to do it. First of all, you have to understand that ejaculation is merely a reflex, which although it's triggered at the same time as orgasm doesn't necessarily have to follow. I'm sure you've already experienced a gag reflex when something's 'gone down the wrong way,' a long cock for example. It's a miracle how some people can push long, thick dicks past their uvula and into the small intestine even though the reflex of the 9th cranial nerve actually ought to prevent this. Well, it works with the help of good faith and regular training. Not faith in the Pope, but in yours truly who has already explained to you in *Blow Me! The Complete Guide to Oral Sex* how to outsmart the gag reflex, and who is now telling you how to interrupt the ejaculation reflex. So here's the long overdue lecture on 'the mechanics of ejaculation.'

While you're drooling over your filthy pictures or DVDs, the seminal filaments are clambering out of your testicles and up into the spermatic ducts. At the same time, the seminal fluid is champing at the bit in the prostate, and last but not least, the Cowper's glands whose clear juice dribbles out of many men's cocks long before they reach orgasm are slavering away. As soon as the arousal has reached its climax, you begin to fidget like a fish out of water, and the whole lot combines and is ejected at top speed and flushed out via the urethra. The rest will be familiar to you. The moment just before the seminal fluid is waved off on its journey into the unknown is called the 'point of no return.' Got that? I bet your biology teacher never told you about that, right? What if you were to make that the subject of your next assignment? It'll provoke a lot of embarrassed laughter in class, but all the gay boys will be after you.

Joking aside, it's vital to understand this mechanism, because if you're already unable to separate orgasm and ejaculation in your head you won't manage it on a physical level either, and you'll always be a wretched one hit wonder. You've already mastered the first of five steps, so let's move on to the exercises:

Step 2: You have to train a muscle whose existence you've hitherto only noticed in awkward situations: the PC (pubococcygeus) muscle. It got its name because it runs from the pubic bone to the coccyx, and one of its jobs is to control the flow of urine. This muscle was automatically trained when human beings didn't yet have chairs and had to squat down and then stand up again 5000 times a day. If you learn to control this muscle, you'll learn to stop your ejaculation. It's a straightforward training program: When you're pissing, inter-rupt it three times without using your stomach or butt muscles. It's very unpleasant to start with, especially if you already have prostate problems, but that will decrease over time; it gets easier and easier.

Once you've familiarized yourself with your PC in this way you can also train it when you're not peeing, preferably in the morn-ing immediately after you've woken up. Tense, relax, tense, relax ... three sets of 15. If you do that three times a day you'll strengthen the muscle faster.

Once you've mastered that, increase the exercise: Tense the PC and hold it for a whole five seconds every time. Repeat this 15 times too. Three sets three times daily and you'll soon manage it.

As soon as you can more or less maintain that, go one step further and try to keep this tension up for 15 seconds while otherwise re-maining totally relaxed. No, that isn't a contradiction. You're relaxed because the rest of your body is meant to stay relaxed while you're doing the exercise, and also because the PC has built up so much strength that tensing it in this way no longer requires any effort.

And why should 15 seconds be your goal? Because that corre-sponds to the approximate duration of the ejaculation reflex, so you must learn to maintain it if you'd like to experience an orgasm without ejaculating.

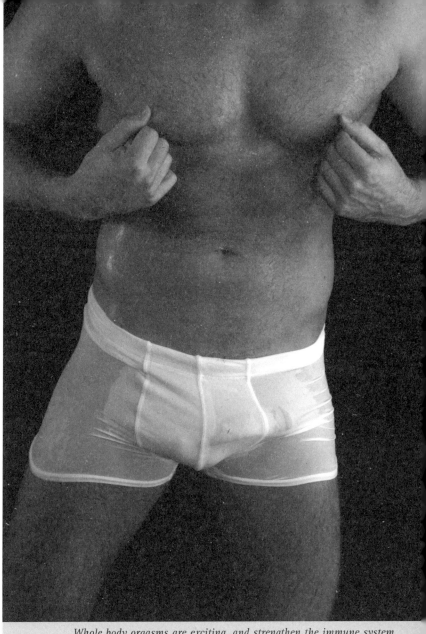

Whole body orgasms are exciting, and strengthen the immune system.

Moreover, Tantrics and Taoists also learn how to master similar exercises. Pregnant women who can't hold their wee learn how to combat this via so-called Kegel exercises (named for Dr. Arnold Kegel who developed them in the 1950s), and they're identical to the procedure outlined above.

Step 3: Now you have to become more aware of your arousal curve. That means: You should no longer allow yourself to simply be driven by that hot feeling until the fireworks go off in your cock (followed by snoring), but examine what's happening instead. Surf the wave of your arousal and learn to recognize the milestones on the way to orgasm. What happens at what point of your arousal? When do your nipples protrude? When do your legs begin to twitch? At what point does your breathing change? In what way? And is there any change inside your head (pressure increases, a warm feeling, seeing stars)? The most important thing is to switch your night vision to super-high resolution every time just before you cum. You must learn to recognize all your physical reactions at this moment, because they'll help you to know when to intervene.

That's why it's preferable during this research phase to not allow yourself to be distracted by porn movies and the like, so that you can devote all your attention to your body and its sensations. Once you notice you're about to cum, use the above-mentioned delay techniques in order to get closer and closer to the famous 'point of no return.'

Um ... you won't succeed right away. You won't have learnt it after five or fifteen times jerking off either, so be patient. Be satisfied if you learn a little more about yourself with every solo performance. Approach the issue in a spirit of playfulness and curiosity. If you just want to crack it quickly, it'll be tiring and there's a big risk you'll abandon it in frustration.

Step 4: Now you have to learn how to tense your PC muscle at precisely the right time. A couple of seconds too early and you'll prevent orgasm. A couple of seconds too late and you'll no longer be able to suppress the reflex, and any chance of further orgasms has been missed. The right time is the moment immediately before the muscles at the base of your cock begin to contract in order to expel the sperm. Maintain the tension for 10 to 15 seconds, and the ejaculation reflex is suppressed, you sense orgasm, and your stiffy is still in place. Carry on! Your sex partners will truly be amazed.

One nice side effect: If you don't waste the pent-up energy in the form of a genital orgasm (i.e. ejaculate), a whole body orgasm can be achieved, ideally a spiritual one where you feel you're becoming one with your partner (or with the world). Cool, huh?

▼ Practice makes perfect

As I've said, it's all very straightforward; you just have to practice. You need a maximum of six months to master this technique.

However exciting multi-orgasms may be, you can even go one better, namely never ejaculate again. Taoists don't practice multi-orgasmic sex to dispel boredom, but to reinforce their health. The idea behind this is that the body can't tell the difference between ejaculating for fun and ejaculating to procreate, so your organs do their best every time you squirt to create new life.

That sounds pretty serious. But once you experience the exhaustion that sets in after the big 'oh,' you'll be more inclined to concede this point. Some sects in India thus drink their own sperm to re-ingest the 'wasted energy'; after all, it contains minerals, enzymes and vitamins. However, the energy is still lost.

Mantak Chia (one of the leading instructors in Taoist sexuality here in the West) writes that a man who has sexual intercourse without spilling his seed strengthens his vital substance. If he does it twice, his sight and hearing become more acute. If he manages it three times, all his physical ailments will disappear; four times, and he will begin to find his inner peace. After the fifth time his blood will circulate strongly; the sixth time, and his genitals will acquire extraordinary abilities. Seven times, and his thighs and buttocks will become firm. Eight times, and his body will display radiant health. Nine times, and his life expectancy increases.

I'd say that should be taken metaphorically, but the gist is clear: Cumming without ejaculating has a health-promoting aspect.

Tao – the doctrine of the path

'Dao' means 'path,' and in classic Chinese it also means 'method,' 'principle' or 'right path.' Ever since Lao Tse (a legendary Chinese thinker who supposedly lived in the 6th century BC) it has described an all-pervasive principle which underlies the world as we know it, from which the 'ten thousand things,' the cosmos and its order emerge. The Tao is not seen as a being (god), but as the origin and the reconciliation of opposites. On the one hand it creates duality (light and shade, day and night, man and woman, yin and yang), and on the other hand it encompasses this duality. The entire world is then created from their transformation, movement and interaction.

The crowning glory of lust: multiple orgasms.

When I was attempting to acquire these techniques I suffered from headaches, ended up with 'blue balls,' and could no longer sleep properly due to all the energy I had. They're phenomena that occur if you don't know how to deal with the energies produced by dry orgasms. This involves much more than a little PC muscle training, and since my experience in such matters is somewhat limited I've sought the advice of someone who's been practicing and teaching this for some years now: Julian is a sociologist and Shiatsu practitioner who lives with his wife in Berlin.

Harder, more often, healthier

Julian, what have I been doing wrong?
If you play around with arousal, your body assumes you're wanting to create new life, so it builds up lots of energy which is discharged when you ejaculate. Yet if you don't ejaculate, it accumulates in the testicles, which begin to hurt; it's known as 'blue balls.'

I've tried to get the energy to circulate (as described by Chia*), but have only suffered from headaches.
If you've gotten headaches, the energy is presumably not circulating but accumulating in your head instead.

What should I have done differently?
You must learn to allow the energy to circulate throughout your body so that it's resupplied to the organs, which are thereby strengthened. In order to do this you must be aware of the small energy cycle and the big energy cycle, and learn how to master them.

How do I do that?
It's not entirely risk-free to learn about that from reading alone,
if you don't have a teacher who can point out your mistakes. Individual organs might 'overheat.'

Doctors would describe a statement like that as sheer humbug!
Sure. But the Tao isn't about validating or refuting scientists. Taoists proceed in an empirical fashion: Feel, and you'll know what's true. If this philosophy, this way of life works for you, then practice it. If not, don't.

So does an orgasm without ejaculation feel different to one with?
In Taoism one responds to this question with a metaphor: If you compare the ejaculation-based orgasm to a meat dish, the orgasm without ejaculation is not only a meat-free dish, but a vegetarian one. You have to 'cook' in a completely different way. In other words: If ejaculating is no longer the purpose of sex, this opens up an entirely new sphere. The significance of (and reason for) sexual activity must be reconsidered.

 And yes, it feels different. If I don't ejaculate, the orgasmic feeling lasts longer. The whole body prickles and tingles afterwards. Sometimes I still have shivers running down my spine hours after sex. It only lasts for a short while if I satisfy my horniness and ejaculate, whereas I can benefit from multiple orgasms for ages. But Taoist practices don't only aim at sexual gratification.

So what else?
Sexuality is just a small part of the Taoist doctrine. Essentially it's a way of acquiring/maintaining health and spirituality: How can I make better use of nutrition, strengthen my bones and achieve peace of mind? Some Taoists also see this as the key to immortality, and in order to achieve this the body has to be cleansed and purified and its energy increased. Hardcore Taoists totally avoid ejaculation since it requires a great deal of strength.

Immortality?
The strength we've inherited from our forefathers, the strength that's passed on with the seed during procreation, resides in the kidneys and sexual organs. Once it's been used up, we die. On the other hand, if it's preserved it helps to strengthen the body, which can thus remain healthy and flexible into old age. You can achieve immortality via lifelong training in solitude, but

it's enough for me to use this knowledge to keep healthy into old age.

Don't you get the feeling you're missing out on something without ejaculation?
No. An orgasm that 'fuels' the whole body is much more satisfying and fulfilling than one that's restricted to the genitals. If you've never had this experience you'll find it hard to imagine, but if you have you'll no longer miss ejaculation. Quite the opposite: Sex without ejaculation becomes a pleasure. However, ejaculation can also have a somewhat cleansing element to it. Men who live in big cities accumulate toxins which need to be rinsed out from time to time so that the sperm can renew itself—assuming they're strong and healthy. If they're sick, old, or feel run down, they shouldn't be wasting yet more energy.

This is precisely the argument of many urologists: Frequent ejaculation protects you from inflammations and even cancer.
In order to prevent cancer and inflammations, it's better to increase your energies and thereby strengthen the immune system; after all, that's much more logi-

cal. Taoism has far more efficient ways of eradicating tension or cleansing the prostate. One particular way of peeing (training the PC muscle) stops you from getting an enlarged prostate. You can massage away any tension in the balls.

If these practices are so awesome, why are they still considered to be 'secret knowledge'?
The credo of Christian morality is that there's something diabolical about sex, hence this secrecy, the taboo, and the shame. And things that aren't talked about can't be developed any further. Sex has always been something precious and sacred for Taoists; after all, sexual energy is always there. That's why it's not taboo in Taoism to discuss this or teach these practices. On the contrary: Sex exists to make you strong and healthy, as well as to allow spiritual growth.

How did people actually hit on the idea of developing these techniques? Was someone a bit bored?
No (*laughs*). These techniques were developed thousands of years ago by shamans in China who were searching for ways to become immortal. Since they were very practical, they devoted themselves to the strongest form of energy that's available to us: sexual energy. Later on, men who belonged to the upper class began to marry several women at once, not so they could form a harem, but so they could live together polygamously. The wives weren't there to satisfy the man; the man had to be able to satisfy all the women he married. If he couldn't manage that, he lost face. Not being able to do it anymore after the first orgasm could therefore have serious consequences, and as you know, the refractory period gets longer as you grow older. So alternative practices had to be developed so that men could fulfill their marital obligations. This included training in specific thrusting techniques whereby men could satisfy their wives more effectively, but also developing the ability to have multiple orgasms.

* Mantak Chia and Douglas Abrams Arava:
The Multi-Orgasmic Man: Sexual Secrets Every Man Should Know

▼ Jerk-off material #2

Now all I need to do is answer the question of what you get up to while you're experiencing ever higher surges of arousal, and occasionally dipping into the land of orgasms. Should you use jerk-off material? No, definitely not. If you're truly going to pay attention to your arousal and above all be able to enjoy it, it's sufficient (nay obligatory) to focus on yourself.

▼ Learning more

If you'd like to learn more about multiple orgasms, you should consider attending a course. The following links can help you with this:

▶ www.gaylovespirit.com
▶ www.eroticmassage.com

Um ... I've just got a few more questions

Twelve orgasms within half an hour can be fairly exhausting ...

▼ I have problems getting an erection; what can I do about that?

Look for the causes. Maybe you simply don't want sex anymore, and just believe you ought to have more sex because everyone's constantly talking about it. Gay men generally have slightly too much sex rather than too little. So just take a break for a couple of days. Or perhaps you've been relying on excessively strong external stimuli for too long? In that case you might have to wean yourself off them first and rediscover the pleasure you can derive from your own body. Play with yourself, as described above. However, if you're horny and you can't get a hard-on, you should ask a doctor whether it might be linked to medication you're taking (heart medication, antidepressants, anti-virals ...) or whether it has physical causes (diabetes or similar).

▼ Should I jerk off even if I don't want sex?

Absolutely not. Unlike food, drink or air, sex isn't necessary for your survival, so you should only jack off if you want to. But it definitely doesn't do any harm if you spend some time on the practices I've described in Section 5, even if you don't want sex. If that then gives you the urge, so much the better!

▼ How much is 'too often'?

You may already have a problem if you're asking yourself this question, because then the issue is not how often you should/can/must jerk off, but what's preventing you from discovering the right level for yourself. Another criterion is whether the frequency of your jerking off is having a negative impact on your life. Are you putting yourself, your job, your career, your relationships, your family in danger because of this? Or are you harming/injuring yourself as a result? Are you exposing yourself to risks? If none of that applies, enjoy your body and your sensuality. One thing's for sure: 'Too much' jerking has never started any wars.

▼ Will jerking off make my cock bigger?

Yes and no. Some people claim that lots of masturbation will make your cock bigger, but only in childhood because your cock is fully grown once you reach 18 unless you use natural enlargement meth-

Seek advice if you feel the desire but can't get a hard-on.

ods (see below). On the other hand, a cock that isn't used (for sex I mean) does actually shrink.

▼ Am I a pervert because I ...?

Perversion (from the Latin *perversus* = 'reversal,' 'twisting') is the technical term for sexual preferences and practices that deviate from the current social norm. However, the joke is that this 'norm' is in a constant state of flux. You don't need to worry about it so long as you enjoy your favorite practice, nobody's hurt, and you don't suffer any sort of disadvantage as a result. If you're still concerned, discuss it with a doctor, a gay advice service, or a gay-friendly therapist. Talking is the first stage in the healing process!

▼ Is it bad to jerk off on my own, even though I have a partner?

Berlin-based therapist Florian Klampfer has specialized in counseling gay couples, and is familiar with this question from his practice: "For some people, their world collapses when they find out that their partner masturbates on his own. They're afraid that the sexuality they experience together isn't enough (anymore), and/or they feel excluded. Particularly in very close relationships, this can be just as hurtful as cheating on your partner." Yet this rules out something that's crucial for relationships: your own territory, "an area that only belongs to you and to which no one else has access." However, this is absolutely necessary to create your own identity and for your own maturing process, and it directly influences things that are shared. "In other words: Only if you develop yourself and have your own 'secrets' can you also grow within the relationship."

▼ Should I get circumcised?

Circumcision well and truly changes your sex life. Be aware that you might always need lube to jerk off if you have the entire foreskin removed, which means jerking off under the desk at school or even a quickie in the bathroom will no longer be quite as uncomplicated. You can of course take a retrospective look at your last 200 jerk-offs and decide whether they would all have been fine even if you'd had to use lube. Just think of the consequences: tube always in hand, needing to wipe it off, making a mess of clothes.

Advocates of circumcision hereabouts are keen to present it as a matter of survival. They talk about lack of cleanliness and even cancer, as if soap had never been invented. As for the visual perspective: An erect cock only rarely has the foreskin covering the glans in any case, because on most men it pulls back completely. If you're bothered in everyday life about 'cleanliness' or the feeling of being circumcised, you can try the following. It works really well, depending on the type of cock (grower or shower):

▼ How to get rid of your foreskin

Pull your foreskin all the way back. Place your fingers roughly one centimeter below the glans (like a collar around the shaft), and then shove the foreskin over your fingers. If you now remove your fingers from underneath the foreskin, a kind of 'skin pocket' is created, which remains behind the edge of the glans—so long as you don't get an erection. In this way you can experience what being circumcised feels like in everyday life; even peeing works really well like this. The biggest problem: The bare glans is very sensitive in the beginning, and there's a danger you'll get a hard-on. To be precise, you're constantly horny. If you've got the kind of cock that swells up, i.e. that gets really enlarged when it gets hard, the foreskin pulls back and then slips over the glans again when you go soft. So don't immediately give up after the first attempt!

▼ How hot is a cock piercing when you're jerking off?

The answer to this question lies within you, and unfortunately you'll only find it once you've been pierced. I'm not pierced myself, but I've discussed it with lots of people, and this is the impression I get: Purely at the level of sensation, it's very arousing to start with, rather like being circumcised. But soon, maybe within two months, you'll have gotten used to it, so then you need mental stimulation again. If it turns you on to have a ring, rod or clothes hanger pierced through your glans, the answer will doubtless be: "Yes, it's hot." However, there are some accompanying problems and disadvantages: For instance, you'll spray like a watering can when you pee; your sperm will no longer fly through the air with the greatest of ease when you cum, but will merely drip out instead; some men won't allow you to fuck them, even with a condom, or won't want to suck your dick because (not altogether unjustifiably) they're afraid they'll knock

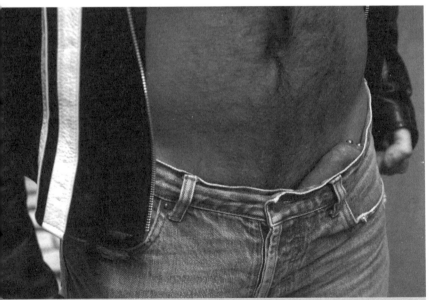

Curisosity: A pierced cock is always an eyecatcher.

their teeth out. However, if you're not put off by all of this, why not head for the nearest piercing studio?

▼ I often feel so empty after I've jerked off. What am I doing wrong?

Either you're still tormenting yourself with feelings of guilt, along the lines of 'anyone who jerks off will go to hell,' or despite any pleasure you might derive from this you miss having another guy to share the joy of orgasm with. The release of hormones can also be responsible for a subsequent sense of sadness and emptiness. You can simply skip the emptiness phase or get someone to join you in bed next time and see if it feels any better.

▼ My cock is too small; how can I make it bigger?

It's claimed that 50% of all men are worried about the size of their penis. For many of them, it's literally a yardstick for their self-esteem, partly because whenever it's talked about in public the scale has no upper limit and men tend to measure in meters rather than centimeters.

First question: What do you consider to be 'too small'? The average is around 14 cm/5.5 inches (erect), so you're in the same boat as approx. 75% of all men if that applies to you. Before you let yourself in for some serious interventions, I'd advise you to check your preconceptions first.

Medication and operations

I wouldn't advise you to turn to 'medication,' because it's only the wallets of the manufacturers and retailers that'll get any bigger. Operations are expensive and not without their dangers.

PenisPlus+

After conducting a little research, the only mechanical enlarger that appears to be at least halfway reputable is PenisPlus+ ▶ www.penisplus.com. However, it's quite a job because you have to remove the stretcher every time you take a leak. And please note what the manufacturer says: "At the rate of stretching for only 8 hours per day, growth is initiated after only a few weeks."

Vacuum pumps

How much length and girth can be gained depends on the strength of the vacuum, how long you use it for each time, the period over which you pump, how regularly you do it, and of course your age and initial size. If you can prove this is really a major issue for you, vacuum pumps can even be prescribed by doctors! So just find yourself an understanding urologist and have a serious discussion with them.

▼ Natural penis enlargement

Aha! So you immediately want to cut to the chase and not have to read the whole of this tiresome book beforehand. After all, it costs money; how very clever of you! You might manage to learn all the following exercises by heart, but just consider that a bigger cock isn't the be-all and end-all. You should also know what to do with it, and this book ended up being so thick because there are an endless number of possibilities. Over 100 pages for holds, techniques and positions alone! Plus exercises that help you to experience whole body orgasms, cum several times, and exploit your horniness to become stronger and healthier. In short: fun for the rest of your life. Surely that's worth the purchase price, so please make your way to the cash desk!

Why make it bigger anyway?

Let's get down to business. The exercises to make your cock bigger are as old as the hills. The Yellow Emperor (China, 2674–2575 BC) is

supposed to have used them, although not because he was encouraged to do so by pornography and the sex industry, as is so often the case today. No, back then it was all about finding ways of properly satisfying women. You might read today that a cock length of 10 centimeters is enough to achieve that (because the clitoris is only a few centimeters above the entrance to the vagina), but that's only half the truth. To be more precise, a third of it. Women don't only reach orgasm by massaging the clitoris, but we won't go into that in any greater depth here—literally.

The enlargement techniques were developed so that the cock would, if required, be able to fit the pussy. Since that's of little relevance to gay men, I could confidently move on to another topic at this juncture, but obviously you still want your cock to be bigger otherwise you wouldn't be reading what's written here. So:

Gay sizes

You don't need a big cock to have gay sex. So long as you can hold it with two fingers and masturbate successfully, it's big enough.

You should learn instead how to make men crazy with your kisses. Train your tongue to lick asses into a state of erotic ecstasy, and then a big cock becomes superfluous. Guys who can only have sex with big dicks are really missing out on something.

▼ The exercises

1. Warm your dick

It's not a good idea to put it in the microwave. It makes more sense to lay a hot water bottle on it—although you can't really wrap it around your cock. Dansex.dk offers the WaterWarmUp, a kind of close-fitting mini hot water bottle that has been specifically developed for this purpose.

We're talking about 'warming up' here, so don't pour boiling water into your lap in the vain hope that 'more is better'. On the contrary. This warming process is only meant to open up the vessels so blood can flow more easily into the erectile tissue: 40°- 45°C is adequate. You should be patient for five minutes, although it won't do any harm either if you want to enjoy the warmth between your legs for 10 minutes.

2. Raise your willy!

Play around with your balls, nipples or earlobes, or think about a changing room full of sweaty construction workers, until your cock begins to fill with blood. The emphasis here is on 'begins'. If it's rock hard, think about all the tax you've paid in your life, and what it's been used for. A good level of arousal is when your cock is filled to the maximum but hasn't yet become erect. Or: like it is once you've cum.

3. Pull it by the ears!

Uncut men should pull the hood back from the head, place their index finger and thumb under the edge of the glans, and then pull/ stretch the cock out until it almost hurts. Fine, and now we reach the most difficult part of this exercise: Hold the thing stretched like this for ten minutes and/or gradually pull it further and further without causing any pain. You should occasionally take a look at your glans. If it's really white, you're squeezing too firmly and no blood is getting through anymore. And for the benefit of those tough guys who are reading this: It won't happen quicker if it hurts. Quite the opposite: You can forget making your cock longer and at best end up with bruising. Do you realize how unappetizing that can be?

Okay, after ten minutes you can relax your little hand again, and your pecker can take a breather too. Knead it a little, and shake it just like you'd shake muscles after exerting yourself. Eager beavers can repeat the exercise after taking a break of at least five minutes.

Naturally it's more convenient to simply hang a weight from your cock so your hands are free—to knit that warm winter muffler, for example. But how do you attach a weight to your glans without completely throttling it? A look at professional penis stretchers will enlighten you: Use a thick nylon cord (washing line), and then all you need is a toggle fastening like you find on jackets, which secures the cord behind your glans. You can plunder suitable weights from household appliances: kettles, mixers, washing machines.

But the same rules apply as if you were using your hands: It shouldn't hurt (yet) when you stretch it, and don't forget to look at your glans! If it looks unconscious, you've cut off the circulation.

You may be wondering how all this is meant to help. The human body reproduces cells as and when required—you can tell that the skin does this simply by looking at obese people; if it weren't for this mechanism, there would eventually be no more room for all that fat.

4. Milk, milk, milk

If you not only want it longer, but thicker too, you'd do best to look for a juicy farmer's boy who's learnt how to milk cows by hand. When he then staggers into the milking parlor at dawn, still half asleep, just place yourself behind a cow and hold your willy out to him. Oh, I'm just dreaming again.

Imagine you've got something in your urethra you'd like to get rid of. Smear lube onto your cock (a silicone-based one will stay slippery for longer). By doing that, your cock will fill up with blood again (to the level described above). Now place your index finger and thumb around the base of your cock like an 'okay' sign, and squeeze with moderate pressure. Your cock should now look slightly darker because the blood is accumulating; the veins might even stand out a little. Push your thumb/finger toward the tip of the glans as if you were milking a teat. The top half of your cock will become dark red and hard. The correct strength can be achieved if you just about avoid any pain. Once you've reached the top with one hand, the cock behind will have filled with blood again. Place the index finger and thumb of your other hand at the base of your cock and now milk it with this hand. Carry on like this for ten minutes, switching hands all the time.

If that makes you horny (which would hardly be surprising) you unfortunately need to take a break. A rock-hard penis can't easily be milked, so just think about your impending visit to the dentist.

What, that makes you even hornier? Good Lord, you really are a pervert. A few words to the wise: Nothing bad will happen if you simply milk away in this fashion. If on the other hand you squeeze as if you were wanting to throttle your cock, it might be too much for the fine capillary vessels and they'll burst, which will make your cock turn black. That isn't going to help it get any bigger.

The alternative to milking is to resort to the good ol' vacuum pump (see above). Buy a good-quality device and use it properly.

5. Warm your dick #2

To finish off with, it's a good idea to repeat the heat treatment so the gain doesn't immediately vanish.

Um ... I've already mentioned that the PC muscle can be of service here. It has all sorts of positive effects on your genital area, and I hope I don't need to repeat that or give you any further instructions because you're already doing the exercises every day. If you're not, I'll tan your hide (although don't take that as an offer).

The only question remaining is how many centimeters you can add by using these exercises. It varies greatly from person to person, but I'd say you could consider yourself lucky if you manage an extra three. If it's five, you've earned a standing ovation. Once your cock has reached a total length of 45 centimeters you should definitely stop.

Okay, and now the (perhaps) disappointing news: In order to see a result, you'll have to repeat these exercises many times. So be patient! Once you've developed a routine it'll be less of a chore than it sounds. Why not do it during the evening news? You might even find a sexy newscaster. Okay, the chances of that aren't great, but you never know. And um ... don't worry, he can't see what you're doing in front of the TV.

PS: You see how much trouble you can avoid by simply being satisfied with the cock you already have?

Finding out more

There are plenty of books about cocks and jacking off; you'll find lots of examples if you peruse the shelves of any decent gay bookstore. I'll restrict myself to listing a few links, which are both entertaining as well as instructive. Have fun surfing!

- ▶ www.condomania.com
- ▶ www.datenschlag.org/english
- ▶ www.eroticrarities.com
- ▶ www.healthystrokes.com
- ▶ www.jackinworld.com
- ▶ www.letsmasturbate.com
- ▶ www.menshealth.com
- ▶ www.mymasturbation.com
- ▶ www.sexinfo101.com
- ▶ www.solotouch.com
- ▶ www.student.com/sexguide
- ▶ www.thegaysexguide.com

Photo credits:

Henning von Berg; www.henning-von-berg.com
Pages 127; 169

FleshBlack images
Pages 23; 37; 47; 50; 59; 71; 87; 90; 93; 96; 98; 100; 111; 122;
124; 131; 136; 140; 145; 153; 156; 163; 166

Giovanni, http://bitesbygiovanni.blogspot.com/
Page 133

Hot House Entertainment; www.hothouse.com
Pages 16; 28; 32; 60; 63; 74; 105; 120; 169

Ohm Phanphiroj; www.ohmphotography.com
Pages 19; 40; 43; 54; 67; 76; 161

Specialty Publications, LLC Photography by Peter Minx
Page 65

www.uknakedmen.com
Pages 12; 14

© Copyright for product photos lies with the manufacturers
(Pages 78 to 84)

the

form